HOW SOCIALIZATION HAPPENS ON THE GROUND: NARRATIVE PRACTICES AS ALTERNATE SOCIALIZING PATHWAYS IN TAIWANESE AND EUROPEAN-AMERICAN FAMILIES

Peggy J. Miller, Heidi Fung, Shumin Lin,
Eva Chian-Hui Chen, and Benjamin R. Boldt

W. Andrew Collins
Series Editor

MONOGRAPHS OF THE SOCIETY FOR RESEARCH IN CHILD DEVELOPMENT

Serial No. 302, Vol. 77, No. 1, 2012

WILEY-
BLACKWELL   *Boston, Massachusetts   Oxford, United Kingdom*

Kurt Fischer
Harvard University

Doran French
Illinois Wesleyan University

Sarah Friedman
CNA Corporation

Douglas Frye
University of Pennsylvania

Andrew Fuligni
University of California, Los Angeles

Susan Graham
University of Calgary

Elena Grigorenko
Yale University

Megan Gunnar
University of Minnesota

Paul Harris
Harvard University

Susan Hespos
Vanderbilt University

Aletha Huston
University of Texas, Austin

Lene Jensen
Clark University

Ariel Kalil
University of Chicago

Melissa Koenig
University of Minnesota

Brett Laursen
Florida Atlantic University

Eva Lefkowitz
Pennsylvania State University

Katherine Magnuson
University of Wisconsin, Madison

Ann Masten
University of Minnesota

Kevin Miller
University of Michigan

Ginger Moore
Pennsylvania State University

David Moshman
University of Nebraska

Darcia Narvaez
University of Notre Dame

Katherine Nelson
City University of New York

Lisa Oakes
University of California, Davis

Thomas O'Connor
University of Rochester

Yukari Okamoto
University of California, Santa Barbara

Robert Pianta
University of Virginia

Mark Roosa
Arizona State University

Karl Rosengren
University of Illinois, Urbana-Champaign

Judith G.Smetana
University of Rochester

Kathy Stansbury
Morehouse College

Steve Thoma
University of Alabama

Michael Tomasello
Max Planck Institute

Deborah Vandell
University of California, Irvine

Richard Weinberg
University of Minnesota

Hirokazu Yoshikawa
New York University

Qing Zhou
Arizona State University

HOW SOCIALIZATION HAPPENS ON THE GROUND: NARRATIVE PRACTICES AS ALTERNATE SOCIALIZING PATHWAYS IN TAIWANESE AND EUROPEAN-AMERICAN FAMILIES

CONTENTS

ABSTRACT

This monograph builds upon our cumulative efforts to investigate personal storytelling as a medium of socialization in two disparate cultural worlds. Drawing upon interdisciplinary fields of study that take a discourse-centered approach to socialization, we combined ethnography, longitudinal home observations, and microlevel analysis of everyday talk to study this problem in Taiwanese families in Taipei and European-American families in Longwood, Chicago. Comparative analyses of 192 hours of video-recorded observations revealed that conversational stories of young children's past experiences occurred in both sites at remarkably similar rates and continued apace across the age span (2,6, 3,0, 3,6, and 4,0), yielding nearly 900 narrations. These and other similarities coexisted with differences in culturally salient interpretive frameworks and participant roles, forming distinct socializing pathways. The Taipei families enacted a didactic framework, prolifically and elaborately narrating and correcting children's misdeeds. They privileged the bystander and listener roles for child participants, whereas the Longwood families privileged the co-narrator role. The Longwood families repeatedly enacted a child-affirming interpretive framework, erasing or downplaying children's misdeeds, accentuating their strengths, accepting their preferences, and lightening stories with humor. Over time, the Taipei and Longwood children participated more actively and developed holistic but divergent senses of problem, reflecting the distinct socializing pathways that they navigated day by day. These findings open a window on how socialization operates on the ground: Socialization through personal storytelling is a highly dynamic process in which redundancy and variation are conjoined and children participate as active, creative, affectively engaged meaning makers.

I. INTRODUCTION

Peggy J. Miller and Heidi Fung

"Narrative is as much part of human nature as breath and the circulation of the blood."

A.S. Byatt On histories and stories: Selected essays (2001)

In recent years, scholars from developmental psychology and allied disciplines have converged on children's narratives, seeking insight into a host of important topics: memory, affect, self and identity, gender, attachment, family dynamics, and narrative itself (e.g., Bamberg, 1997; Daiute & Lightfoot, 2004; Dyson & Genishi, 1994; Emde, Wolf, & Oppenheim, 2003; Engel, 1995; Fiese, 2006; Pratt & Fiese, 2004; Quas & Fivush, 2009). Our interest in narrative stems from a desire to understand the process by which young children, as incipient cultural beings, are socialized into their communities and cultures. We regard socialization as a fundamental problem in developmental cultural psychology (Cole, 1996; Miller, Fung, & Koven, 2007; Rogoff, 2003; Shweder et al., 2006; Wertsch, 1991) and language socialization (Duranti, Ochs, & Schieffelin, 2011; Miller & Hoogstra, 1992; Ochs & Schieffelin, 1984). These kindred interdisciplinary fields, with roots in psychology, anthropology, and linguistics, share the goal of understanding children in context through a focus on cultural activities and discursive practices. We start from the assumption that children are novice meaning-makers, that narrative is a fundamental tool of meaning making, and that cultures consist of historically situated meanings embodied in practices (Bruner, 1990; Miller, 1994; Miller et al., 2007; Miller, Koven, & Lin, 2011; Shweder et al., 2006). From this vantage point, conjunctions of child, narrative, and significant others form potent socializing sites. We want to know what happens in these conjunctions when children grow up in two disparate cultural worlds.

Children gravitate to stories from a remarkably early age. But their caregivers do not hand them narrative with a capital N. Rather, children encounter particular genres of narrative that are practiced in particular ways, reflecting variation within and across local worlds (Miller, Cho, & Bracey, 2005; Ochs & Capps, 2001). In the longitudinal study reported here, we examine narrative practices as a medium of socialization during the preschool years, comparing middle-class Taiwanese families and middle-class European-American families. We are interested in narrative as a means by which interpretive frameworks and modes of participation are made available to and appropriated by young children. By treating narrative as a set of practices that children and caregivers engage in together, we gain access to the process by which children step into and move along alternate socializing pathways (e.g., Miller & Goodnow, 1995; Wiley et al., 1998).

It is likely that children everywhere experience a multiplicity of narrative genres but that the particular mix varies from place to place. Children growing up in the 21st century may encounter written stories, such as fairy tales, fables, children's literature, and religious texts; family stories passed down orally from one generation to the next; and television, video and computer-mediated stories. In addition, many children around the world experience oral-narrative traditions specific to their ethnic, class, or cultural identity, such as Navajo skinwalker stories (Brady, 1984), Native Hawaiian talk-story (Au, 1993), or Kwara-ae (Solomon Island) shaping the mind (Watson-Gegeo & Gegeo, 1990). However, we have chosen to study a genre that is a cultural universal, namely, oral stories of personal experience. These are stories told in conversation in which the narrator invokes an event from his or her past experience.

There is growing evidence that such stories are culturally differentiated from the beginning; wherever personal storytelling occurs with young children, it takes on local color, reflecting and transmitting local interpretive frameworks, affective stances, moral orientations, and modes of participation (e.g., Fivush & Hammond, 1990; Fivush & Nelson, 2006; Fivush & Wang, 2005; Heath, 1983; McCabe & Peterson, 1991; Miller et al., 2005; Miller & Moore, 1989; Ochs & Capps; 2001; Scollon & Scollon, 1981; Sperry & Sperry, 1996, 2000). The primary purpose of this monograph is to contribute to a deeper understanding of the role that diverse personal storytelling practices play in the early socialization process. We build upon and extend a long-term collaborative project that is situated in the first two authors' research teams in the United States and Taiwan.

A second purpose is to contribute to a more general intellectual trend in developmental psychology. In recent years, the problem of understanding children in cultural context has been moving from the periphery to the center of the discipline. This is apparent, for example, in the inclusion of three chapters on culture and development in the *Handbook of Child Psychology* (Damon & Lerner, 2006), the preeminent reference volume in the field, and the publication of *The Child: An Encyclopedic Companion* (Shweder et al., 2009), which showcases the wealth of knowledge now available about the plurality of childhood experiences around the globe. Recognizing this diversity within and across cultures, more and more scholars agree that there are multiple

2

developmental pathways, not a single, universal pathway (e.g., Garcia Coll & Marks, 2009; Göncü, 1999; Greenfield, Keller, Fuligni, & Maynard, 2003; Goodnow, Miller & Kessel, 1995; Shweder et al., 2006; Weisner, 1996). Each pathway is "made up of 'stepping stones' of activities and practices" that are "loosely organized into a daily routine of life, and, in turn, into a 'cultural career'—a way of life that engages the self, identity, and our sense of personhood and meaning" (Weisner, 2002, p. 325).

This trend also has generated an emerging consensus that understanding children in context requires attention to meaning (Briggs, 1998; Chen, Rubin, & Li, 1995; Chen et al., 1998; Cole, 1996; Dyson, 2003; Göncü, 1999; Gottlieb, 2004; Greenfield, Suzuki, & Rothstein-Fisch, 2006; Harkness & Super, 1996; Heath, 1983; Hudley, Haight, & Miller, 2003; Larson & Jensen, 2005; Miller, 1997; Rogoff, 1990, 2003; Shweder, 1991) and has led to a variety of methodological innovations that allow scholars to recoup a deeper and more nuanced understanding of development and culture as intertwined processes (e.g., Duncan, Huston, & Weisner, 2007; Garcia Coll & Marks, 2009; Gaskins, 1999; Jessor, Colby, & Shweder, 1996; Weisner, 2005). The study presented here contributes to this conversation by offering an innovative conceptual and methodological approach that places discursive practices front and center.

The remainder of this chapter is organized as follows. First, we present the theoretical and methodological perspectives that frame our work. Then, we review the specific studies on which the current study builds. The chapter concludes with our research questions and a roadmap to the ensuing chapters.

THEORETICAL AND METHODOLOGICAL FRAMING

Socialization Through Discursive Practices

Discourse-level language has become an important locus of inquiry in a variety of disciplines that have a stake in understanding childhood socialization; these include psychology (Bruner, 1990; Fivush & Haden, 2003; Miller et al., 2007; Nelson & Fivush, 2004; Shweder et al., 2006), psychological anthropology (Briggs, 1998; Fung, 1999; Fung & Chen, 2001; Holland, Lachicotte, Skinner, & Cain, 1998; Quinn, 2005a; Shweder & Much, 1987), and sociology (Corsaro, 2003, 2005). We have been influenced by this interdisciplinary current and especially by the field of language socialization, which originated in linguistic anthropology and developmental psychology in the early 1980s. As its name implies, this field is concerned with the overlap between language and the social world and, especially, with the role that language plays in socializing novices into local meanings. Inspired by Edward Sapir's famous words, "Language is a great force of socialization, probably the greatest that exists" (Mandelbaum, 1951, p. 15), this field rests on the premise that children are

3

not only socialized through language but also socialized to use language (Ochs & Schieffelin, 1984). Another guiding principle is the Vygotskian notion that meanings are created by using language for particular purposes in socially defined activities (Cole, 1996; Vygotsky, 1934/1978; Wertsch, 1985, 1991). If language not only reflects meaning but also constitutes meaning, then an adequate theory of socialization must incorporate language in a principled way (Fung, 1999; Miller, 1994).

But what exactly is meant by language? Scholars from this tradition have contributed to and been influenced by the turn toward practice approaches to language, and thus, they define language very broadly (Hanks, 1996; Ochs, 1990; Ortner, 1984). Terms such as "communicative" or "discursive" practices are used to signal a contrast with a purely referential conception of language, to privilege the analysis of speech events in context, and to encompass levels of organization beyond the sentence. Critically important for current purposes, these larger sequences include speech genres, such as narrative. Practice approaches permit a more comprehensive cultural analysis because cultural principles are expressed not only in the content of talk but also in the way that discourse is organized, enacted, and embedded (see Bauman & Briggs, 1990; Duranti & Goodwin, 1992; Hanks, 1996; Koven, 2007; Miller, 1994; Silverstein, 1976/1995 for extensive discussion of practice approaches to language). These ideas shape the work presented here, leading us to study storytelling as embedded practices whose meanings can best be grasped by taking into account what is said, how it is said, and how children participate.

Although it is beyond the scope of this monograph to review the extensive literature on language socialization, we note here several important insights that are relevant to our project. First, the flow of sociocultural messages is relentless in the myriad communicative interactions of novices' everyday lives (e.g., Miller, 1982; Ochs, 1988; Schieffelin, 1990; Watson-Gegeo & Gegeo, 1999). Second, socialization happens as novices and more experienced persons participate recurrently in local discursive practices. The term "recurrent" (or "routine") is key because it is through repetition that socializing pathways are established (Kulick & Schieffelin, 2004). These practices index tacit organizations of time, space, and social personnel and convey both implicit and explicit socialization messages (Miller & Goodnow, 1995; Miller & Hoogstra, 1992). And, finally, there is enormous diversity within and across cultures in language socialization, including variation in caregivers' ideologies, goals, and values; in practices relating to childrearing and language learning; and in the definition, naming, and practice of specific speech genres (e.g., Duranti et al., 2011; Garrett & Baquedano-López, 2002; Schieffelin & Ochs, 1986). Taken together, these insights motivate our interest in establishing whether personal storytelling occurred *routinely* in Taipei and Chicago, underscore the universal yet variable nature of socialization, and call attention to the duality

4

of the socializing process as deeply implicit yet involving explicit parental goals and ideologies.

Early Socialization Through Narrative Practices

Although the conception of socialization sketched in the preceding section applies to socialization at any point in the lifespan and in any institutional context, our abiding interest is in *early* socialization in the *family* context. We assume that socialization begins at birth, but we follow Vygotsky (1934/1978) in positing that the ontogenetic emergence of language provides a new and powerful socializing tool (see also Cole, 1996; Wertsch, 1985). The age span (2,6 to 4,0) addressed in this monograph represents a period of rapid language development, allowing children to enter into more sophisticated communicative exchanges with family members.

We have already anticipated some reasons why we chose to focus on personal storytelling rather than some other discursive practice. In *Acts of Meaning*, Jerome Bruner (1990) argued that children come into the world "prepared" to use stories to make sense of human action. Youngsters in cribs and high chairs, from working-class and middle-class families, heirs to different ethnic and cultural traditions use narrative to interpret their past experiences (e.g., Heath, 1983; Miller, Cho, & Bracey, 2005; Miller, Hoogstra, Mintz, Fung, & Williams, 1993; Nelson, 1989; Scollon & Scollon, 1981; Sperry & Sperry, 1996). However, we still know little about how early socialization through personal storytelling transpires over extended periods of time in different cultural contexts. The project reported here attempts to remedy this omission. We build on earlier studies (described more fully later in this chapter) with Taipei and Chicago families, in which personal storytelling emerged as a robust practice that already carried culturally salient meanings when the child participants were only 2,6 (Miller, Fung, & Mintz, 1996; Miller, Wiley, Fung, & Liang, 1997). In this monograph, we follow the same children at 3,0, 3,6, and 4,0. To use Weisner's (2002) metaphor, having identified an early stepping stone in each socializing pathway, we sought the next stepping stones.

We also wanted to know how the children would navigate these stepping stones. Language socialization researchers, like developmental psychologists, recognize that young children play an active role in the socialization process. They emphasize the interrelated contributions that child, caregivers, and companions make to the child's socialization through their mutual participation in routine practices. In this view, the child is not a passive individual shaped by socializing agents but an active, constructive, transforming, or resisting person (Miller & Goodnow, 1995; Taylor, 1995; Watson-Gegeo & Gegeo, 1999). A focus on children's participation in narrative practices offers a way to access their meaning making in all its "activeness": in any given narration, a child

5

might reconfigure, playfully alter, add to, question, or challenge what her interlocutors say and do. As the discourse unfolds, researchers can follow in the interpretive footsteps of the child (Briggs, 1998). This way of construing socialization envisions children as navigators of socializing pathways or makers of meaning. We use these terms not only to emphasize the activeness just described but also to signal the holistic nature of this process (Miller & Goodnow, 1995). To navigate a socializing pathway is to engage in a process that is simultaneously cognitive, affective, social, moral, and personal.

Ethnography Plus Analysis of Talk

The study of early socialization through discursive practices is associated with a particular kind of research—ethnography combined with micro-level analysis of talk—that has characterized language socialization research from its inception (Ochs & Schieffelin, 1984). Like all ethnographic research, this approach seeks to understand cultural meanings from the "inside," that is, from the perspectives of the participants themselves, using the tools of participant-observation and interviewing (Briggs, 1986; Jessor, Colby, & Shweder, 1996; Miller, Hengst, & Wang, 2003; Woolcott, 1995). Ethnographic studies begin with a period of fieldwork in which the ethnographer collects background information about the community, hones her facility in the local language(s), and immerses herself in the local scene via participant observation.[1] The distinguishing feature of the version of ethnography adopted by language socialization researchers is the close-up analysis of everyday talk. Researchers make systematic observations of the child in the contexts of everyday life, that is, under conditions that are ecologically valid and culturally appropriate. These observations are audio- or video-recorded and transcribed verbatim in the original language (Ochs, 1979); the transcripts are examined and emic or inductive codes, reflecting local meanings, are derived (Bloom, 1974; Emerson, Fretz, & Shaw, 1995; Gaskins, Miller, & Corsaro, 1992; Pike, 1967). This process of transcription and coding is very time-consuming. In her influential book on language socialization among the Kaluli of Papua, New Guinea, Schieffelin (1990) estimated that it took 27 hr to prepare a transcript of an hour-long audio-taped observation. However, these laborious procedures are necessary to the precision and rigor of the work. If socialization proceeds through discursive practices, it is vitally important that those practices be documented in meticulous detail.

Several other methodological commitments should be noted. In contrast to much research in developmental psychology, research on language socialization has privileged the study of small numbers of children in great depth.[2] This is a principled stance, not just a matter of logistics. In order to understand socialization as a contextualized process that unfolds in real time, there is no substitute for studying discursive practices when, where, and as they happen

(Miller et al., 2011). A closely related feature is a commitment to longitudinal investigation; specific discursive practices are tracked over extended periods of time. The need for a wide temporal window also dovetails with the nature of ethnography as a type of inquiry that requires sustained experience with the participants in order to discern their cultural ways (Becker, 1996).

PERSONAL STORYTELLING AT 2,6 IN TAIPEI AND LONGWOOD

With this theoretical and methodological preamble in place, we review the specific studies on which the current project builds. In the late 1980s and early 1990s, the first two authors and their colleagues conducted a comparative ethnographic study of personal storytelling as a medium of socialization in Taipei and in the *Longwood* (pseudonym) neighborhood of Chicago (Miller, 1996; Miller, Potts, Fung, Hoogstra, & Mintz, 1990; Miller, Sandel, Liang, & Fung, 2001; Miller et al., 1996, 1997). We chose to compare these two groups because the cultures were widely divergent, and, at the time, no research existed on young children's personal storytelling in any Chinese culture. We also had the practical advantage that our team included individuals with native cultural and linguistic expertise in either Taiwan or the United States.

Following the research model outlined in the previous section (see Chapter II for a detailed description of our methods), we made our first recorded observations of everyday interactions in the home when the focal children were 2,6. We transcribed and analyzed these recordings to determine whether the Taipei and Longwood families told stories of young children's past experiences. The answer was a resounding yes. Furthermore, these stories occurred at remarkably similar rates, about four per hour on average. This initial analysis thus established that personal storytelling was a routine practice in both sites (Miller et al., 1996, 1997).

A Culturally Salient Interpretive Framework in Taipei

From a language socialization perspective, when a genre occurs recurrently in children's everyday lives, it has socializing potential (Kulick & Schieffelin, 2004; Miller, 1994). This led us to ask whether personal storytelling embodied culturally salient meanings in Taipei and Longwood. When we scrutinized the two sets of stories side by side, we discovered a dramatic disparity: the child protagonist was cast as a transgressor in .35 of the Taipei stories, compared with only .07 in Longwood. This five-fold difference favoring the Taipei families was our first piece of evidence that the two sets of stories carried different meanings. But given the practice perspective on narrative presented earlier, this difference in the baseline frequencies of story content was only the first step in an investigation of their meanings; we proceeded

7

to take a closer look at the subset of transgression stories in the two cultural cases and conducted microlevel analyses of specific transgression stories.

These analyses revealed differences in the structure, function, and manner of transgression stories (Miller et al., 1996, 1997). The Taipei families were much more likely than their Longwood counterparts to use personal storytelling didactically and to treat children's past transgressions as a pedagogical resource. They talked openly about children's past misdeeds in front of siblings and guests, extracted confessions, and reiterated the rule that had been violated. For example, Didi's mother initiated a story about what happened when he went along to his older sister's music lesson. She asked Didi a question, prompting him to relate that the teacher did not give him a sticker (a reward). She then asked, ". . . then what did you do?" to which he responded, "I then cried." Didi's admission led his sister to chime in, "Cried loudly, 'Waah! Waah! Waah!'" In the succeeding turns, Didi's mother quoted and enacted Didi's shameful behavior, said that he made her lose face, and added, "I wanted to dig my head into the ground. Right?" while smiling and shaking her head at Didi. Another example, conarrated by Angu and her primary caregiver, revolved around two misdeeds: Angu wrote on the wall and then lied about it. This elaborate story involved more than 100 turns at talk (see Miller et al., 1996). These and other Taipei stories were constructed to establish the child's misdeed as the point of the story, and some ended with lengthy didactic codas, in which a family member articulated the implications of the story for the present or the future.

When the transgression stories were examined in their interactional contexts, a related finding emerged. Many of the Taipei children's transgression stories were immediately preceded by a misdeed in the here-and-now (Miller et al., 1997). In other words, a family member treated the 2-year-old's *current* misdeed as an opportunity to remind him or her of a *previous* misdeed, thereby reinforcing and personalizing moral lessons through concrete exemplars. This practice instantiates the indigenous notion of *jihui jiaoyu* or "opportunity education" identified by Fung (1999). As explained by the Taipei mothers, opportunity education refers to the idea that the most effective way to instill virtues is to seek every opportunity to situate moral lessons in the young child's concrete experience. From this standpoint, parents would be remiss if they allowed children's misdeeds to occur without pedagogical comment. We concluded that the Taipei families were operating with a salient interpretive framework or cultural lens that rendered young children's misdeeds highly narratable for their didactic potential.

Further support for the cultural salience of a didactic interpretive framework can be found in Fung's work on the socialization of shame (Fung, 1999; Fung & Chen, 2001) and Haight's on pretend play (Haight, Wang, Fung, Williams, & Mintz, 1999) in the same Taiwanese families. Even the gestured narratives created by linguistically isolated deaf children in Taiwan carried echoes of a didactic bias (Van Deusen-Phillips, Goldin-Meadow, & Miller, 2001). Looking beyond Taiwan, Beijing mothers, compared with American mothers, exhibited a greater concern with moral rules and moral correctness when conarrating elicited narratives with their 3- and 6-year-olds (Wang & Leichtman, 2000; Wang, Leichtman, & Davies, 2000). And, working-class mothers in Nanjing, China were vigilant in monitoring their children's past and present transgressions in the home context (Wang, Bernas, & Eberhard, 2008). More generally, our findings fit well with Li's (2002, 2004a, 2004b) research on Confucian-based models of learning as a moral process, imbued with purpose, undertaken according to the virtues of diligence, persistence, and humility, and encompassed by the larger project of self-perfection.

A Culturally Salient Interpretive Framework in Longwood

Turning now to the Longwood families, their very low frequency of narrating children's transgressions was even more striking in light of the pedagogical elaboration of such misdeeds in Taiwan. Although Longwood children, like 2-year-olds everywhere, sometimes violated rules of conduct, their families systematically edited these misdeeds out of the narrative record. We called this a "child-favorability bias" (Miller et al., 1996, 1997).

Microlevel examination of the Longwood exceptions, that is, the small set of stories, in which children's misdeeds were narrated, revealed that these stories were not used didactically. Rather, families framed children's misdeeds as humorous or portrayed children in a positive light despite their wrongdoing. For example, one of the longest transgression stories from the Longwood corpus involved a past event, in which Patrick went shopping with his family and was promised a ride on a mechanical horse if he behaved well. Although Patrick misbehaved, he caught himself in time, and thus the point of the story, as narrated by his mother, was that he had behaved well and was rewarded with the promised ride. In another example, the focal child and his older sibling conarrated a story, in which they were punished because they had been "bad boys." But neither one could remember what they had done wrong. When their mother joined in the conversation, she commented ironically, "My kids being bad?!" thereby making light of her sons' misbehavior. She confirmed that the incident had happened the previous week, but she too could not remember what they had done wrong. We argued that this practice of downplaying transgressions in the narrative medium was part of a larger set of practices—conducting serious discipline in private, avoiding invidious comparisons—that the Longwood parents used to protect children's self-esteem and well-being (Miller et al., 1996, 1997).

Interviews with the Longwood mothers supported this interpretation. Although we did not set out to study self-esteem, the mothers brought up self-esteem when discussing childrearing. They placed a very high value on fostering their children's self-esteem and stressed the importance of disciplining in a manner that would not damage their self-esteem (Miller et al., 2001; Mintz, 1999). These findings are consistent with growing evidence that parents from European-American communities subscribe to a folk theory of childrearing that places a much greater premium on cultivating children's self-esteem, compared with parents in Taiwan (Cho, Miller, Sandel, & Wang, 2005; Miller, Wang, Sandel, & Cho, 2002), China and Japan (Stevenson et al., 1990; Stevenson & Stigler, 1992; Tamis-LeMonda, Wang, Koutsouvanou, & Albright, 2002), Puerto Rico (Harwood, Miller, & Irizarry, 1995; Harwood, Schoelmerich, Schulze, & Gonzalez, 1999; A. Miller & Harwood, 2002), and Greece (Tamis-LeMonda et al., 2002).

In sum, using a combination of baseline frequencies of occurrence, qualitative microlevel analysis of stories and interviews with parents, we found that telling stories about young children's past experiences occurred routinely in Longwood and Taipei when the children were 2,6, but that the Taipei families were much more likely to narrate children's past experience from a didactic perspective, the Longwood families from a child-affirming perspective. Although our research was the first to establish that these contrasting interpretive frameworks were used to narrate young children's experience, other studies support the cultural salience of moral education and child-affirmation in Taiwan and the United States, respectively.

RESEARCH QUESTIONS FOR THE CURRENT STUDY

The project reported here expands our earlier work longitudinally and conceptually. Our overarching goal is to ascertain the nature of personal storytelling as an everyday socializing practice in Taipei and Longwood during the period from 2,6 to 4,0. This involved the following specific extensions of our previous work.

Did Personal Storytelling Continue From 2,6 to 4,0?

The most fundamental question arising from our findings at 2,6 is this: Did personal storytelling continue to be practiced routinely, forming socializing pathways? There are several reasons why we expected an affirmative answer. First, telling stories of personal experience was a valued practice in both sets of families; in interviews, the Longwood and Taipei mothers spoke in very favorable terms about personal storytelling, remembered hearing such stories from their parents when they were growing up, and thought it was important for their own children to hear family members tell stories (Miller et al., 2001). In other words, personal storytelling was not reserved for the very young but was valued as a family practice for people of all ages. In addition, since casting 2-year-olds as narrative protagonists was already established as a routine practice, it seemed unlikely that older family members or the children themselves would turn away from this practice as the children became more able narrators and listeners.

Did Personal Storytelling Continue to Carry Culture-Specific Interpretive Frameworks?

Still another reason to expect that personal storytelling would continue during the preschool years is that it already bore the weight of culturally significant interpretive frameworks. LeVine and Norman (2001) have argued that during infancy and early childhood, parents tend to promote behaviors that they regard as consistent with their culture's models of virtue, giving children "a head start" in becoming virtuous according to local standards. They say further that "[parents] are successful enough on average that their children manifest selected behaviors at a 'precociously' early age by the standards of other cultures with different concepts of virtue" (p. 84). Following LeVine and Norman (2001), we suggest that at 2,6, personal storytelling served as a medium through which the Taipei and Longwood families began to deliver a "head start" in becoming virtuous: instilling moral standards and promoting self-improvement in the former and protecting children's psychological well-being and promoting self-affirmation in the latter. We expected that the families would continue to enact these interpretive frameworks through the preschool years, establishing pathways that extended and solidified the head start that began at 2,6 and producing different kinds of precocity in the children. We broke down this expectation into two questions, corresponding to the interpretive frameworks privileged in each site.

Did the Taipei Families Continue to Enact a Didactic Framework?

As presented earlier, the Taipei families were much more likely than their Longwood counterparts to treat youngsters' past transgressions as a didactic resource. Moreover, a didactic interpretive framework was apparent at several levels of narrative analysis. In this monograph, we applied these same codes, adapted slightly for the later ages. This analysis hews most closely to the earlier reports, in which the codes were first developed but extends the analysis to 3,0, 3,6, and 4,0.

Did the Longwood Families Continue to Enact a Child-Affirming Framework?

Unlike the Taipei families, the Longwood families systematically deleted young children's past transgressions from the narrative record. In the current study, we wanted to know whether this child-favorability bias would continue at 3,0, 3,6, and 4,0.

Our microlevel analyses at 2,6 also revealed that on the rare occasion that Longwood families narrated a young child's past misdeed, they downplayed the transgression, mitigated it, treated it humorously, or otherwise made light of it. Along with the narrative erasure of misdeeds, these analyses suggest that one way that Longwood families cast young children in a positive light was by excluding or downplaying the negative. Another way might be to highlight, inflate, or celebrate the positive. This reasoning led us to develop a new coding scheme (see Chapter III) to explore whether the Longwood families were more inclined than the Taipei families to accentuate the positive when narrating children's past experiences. Although the new codes were intended to flesh out the emic interpretive framework associated with Longwood, we also expected that the application of these codes to the Taipei corpus would bring to light dimensions of meaning that were not captured via the didactic codes. The new codes were applied to the entire narrative corpus (2,6, 3,0, 3,6, 4,0) in both sites.

What Kind of Participant Roles Did the Children Enact?

This question takes us into a conceptual and empirical territory that we did not explore in our analyses of the Taipei and Longwood stories at 2,6. As explained earlier, a practice approach to narrative implies that meaning is conveyed in a host of ways that transcend narrative content. This opens up many possibilities for extending our account of personal storytelling beyond interpretive frameworks. We chose to focus on participant roles (Goffman, 1979), that is, the normative expectations that govern how different categories of persons participate in talk. Studies of narrative socialization in diverse cultures reveal substantial variation in children's participant roles. For example, children may be cast as narrators, co-narrators, bystanders, and/or listeners (e.g., Basso, 1996; Fung & Chen, 2001; Miller, 1994; Ochs & Capps, 2001; Ochs & Taylor, 1992; Peterson, 2004; Watson-Gegeo & Gegeo, 1990).

More to the point, there is emerging evidence of different cultural models of communicative style in Taiwan and the United States, with listening being more highly valued than speaking in the former (e.g., Fung, Miller, & Lin, 2004; Gao, 1998; He, 2001; Yum, 1991). Thus, we ask what kinds of participant roles were available to the Taipei and Longwood children? And how did their participation in personal storytelling change during the preschool years? These questions not only enrich our description of how personal storytelling was practiced in the two sites but also raise the question of how interpretive frameworks and participant roles fit together over time to form socializing pathways. Is there an affinity between the listening role and the didactic framework or between the co-narrator role and the child-affirming framework? To our knowledge, there is very little, if any, research that examines interpretive frameworks and participant roles as twin dimensions of socializing pathways.

The issue of participant roles also connects to other developmental work that has not focused on narrative, but which reveals cultural variation in listening/observing versus verbal instruction as modes of learning (Gaskins & Paradise, 2010; Rogoff, 2003). A well-known example comes from Greenfield and Child's work in a Zinacatec Mayan community in Mexico, where children learn to weave through observation (Childs & Greenfield, 1980; Greenfield, 1984). In such cases, children move from quiet observation to full participation when they are ready and/or called on to help with ongoing adult activities (Lave & Wenger, 1991; Rogoff, 2003). The high premium placed on listening and observing is often congruent with other cultural values, for example, respect for elders (Harkness & Super, 1977) or the belief that children's development unfolds "naturally" without parental intervention (Gaskins, 1996, 1999).

How Did the Children Navigate Personal Storytelling and Make Meaning Over Time?

The final analysis presented in this monograph evolved directly out of the findings reported in Chapters III and IV, and thus it cannot be introduced without anticipating those findings. We discovered that personal storytelling did, indeed, continue and that the Taipei and Longwood families continued to enact different cultural biases. Comprised of interpretive frameworks and participant roles, these biases held steady across the whole age range, forming distinct socializing pathways. It is within these respective "holding patterns" that the children evolved as narrative participants and meaning-making persons. Our primary goal in this analysis is to track particular children over time, bringing the holistic process of meaning making into sharper focus. We ask, how did the children navigate personal storytelling, and how did their meaning making change over time? We pursue these questions through microlevel analyses of stories, taking into account the immediate interactional context as well as the repetition of stories.

ROADMAP TO THE MONOGRAPH

In keeping with the theoretical and methodological approach outlined above, Chapter II introduces the worlds in which the children were growing up. We describe these sites as historically situated, sociocultural landscapes, based upon documentary research, and sketch everyday family life, based on ethnographic fieldwork. The methods for the study are also presented in Chapter II. With this ethnographic background in place, the results chapters unfold as follows: frequency of personal storytelling and interpretive frameworks in Chapter III, participant roles in Chapter IV, and children navigating stories in Chapter V. Each of these distinct but related sets of analyses encompasses data at 2,6, 3,0, 3,6, and 4,0, and each results chapter concludes with its own discussion. An overarching discussion is provided in Chapter VI.

Throughout this monograph, readers will find many stories. These are used to clarify how codes were defined, to complement frequency tables, and to delve more deeply into cultural similarities and differences through microlevel analysis of selected examples. Chapter V is based entirely on qualitative analysis of stories. By leavening the text with stories, we hope that readers will get a sense of the ubiquity of stories in Longwood and Taipei, of their different cultural hues, and of the intricacy of the messages they conveyed.

NOTES

1. Ethnographic inquiry was invented more than a century ago as a systematic form of inquiry into cultures distant from one's own (Leeds-Hurwitz, 2005; Malinowski, 1922), and it remains the gold standard in cultural anthropology. As ethnographic methods got taken up in other disciplines, a host of variants evolved; this is true even within developmental psychology (e.g., Chase, 2008; Garcia Coll & Marks, 2009; Göncü, 1999; Jessor et al., 1996; LeVine et al., 1994; Rogoff et al., 1993). In other words, like quantitative methods, ethnographic methods encompass a great many versions and techniques, reflecting specific intellectual histories and traditions (e.g., Denzin & Lincoln, 2005; Miller et al., 2003). Despite this variety, the common goal of ethnographic methods is to represent participants' meanings from their own perspective, as reflecting locally shared meanings. A critical challenge in this endeavor is to avoid mistaking one's own ethnocentric understandings for those of the study participants (Clark, 2003; Corsaro & Miller, 1992; Denzin & Lincoln, 2005; Erickson, 1986; Hammersley & Atkinson, 1995; Jessor et al., 1996; Miller et al., 2003; Wolcott, 1995).

2. For example, Schieffelin's (1990) study was based on four children, each of whom was observed on 7–10 occasions during the period from 2,0 to 2,6, for a total of 83 hr of observations and 33,079 utterances.

II. STUDYING PERSONAL STORYTELLING IN TAIPEI AND LONGWOOD

Heidi Fung, Peggy J. Miller, Shumin Lin, and Eva Chian-Hui Chen

The study was conducted in the late 1980s and early 1990s in two large cities on opposite sides of the globe, Taipei, Taiwan, and Chicago, Illinois. It was part of a larger comparative project that investigated personal storytelling as a medium of socialization in Taiwanese and European-American families. In addition to the longitudinal component reported here, the project included cross-sectional (Miller et al., 1990; Miller, Mintz, Fung, Hoogstra, & Potts, 1992) and interview components (Fung, 1999; Miller et al., 2001; Mintz, 1999). Throughout this monograph, we use the pseudonym Longwood to refer to the Chicago neighborhood in which the study was conducted. As will be described more fully below, Taipei is not organized into neighborhoods, and thus we use the term Taipei when referring to our Taiwanese field site.

To familiarize readers with these two very different worlds, we begin this chapter with a sketch of Taipei and Longwood as historically situated, geopolitical spaces. Then we introduce the families in terms of their "social addresses." The next section presents the design and methods of the study, beginning with the fieldwork and recruitment of families. The chapter concludes with a brief description of everyday family life and parental folk theories in the two sites. In short, this chapter presents the ethnographic background and overview of methods. Specific analytic codes are reserved for the succeeding results chapters (Chapters III–V).

TAIPEI AND LONGWOOD: A BIRD'S EYE VIEW

The capital and largest city in Taiwan, Republic of China, Taipei underwent remarkable economic, social, and political change in the 20th century. During the Japanese colonial period (1895–1945), the Taiwanese experienced serious discrimination and hardship, particularly during World War II. Local Taiwanese languages were suppressed and Japanese was designated the national language. Nevertheless, under colonial rule, Taipei grew into a major metropolis with a modern infrastructure. After World War II, the Japanese

15

government handed Taiwan over to the Chinese Nationalists (also known as the Kuomintang or KMT). In 1947, popular discontent with the KMT's "iron hand" government (Kerr, 1965) and its inept management of the economy, led to a political uprising, the February 28 Incident, in which thousands of Taiwanese died. In 1949, after losing the civil war to the Chinese communists, the Chinese Nationalist government, under Chiang Kai-Shek, retreated to Taipei, bringing with it about two million immigrants from mainland China. At this point Taiwan was demoralized, economically devastated, and heavily dependent on foreign aid.

Considering itself the Chinese government in exile, the KMT aggressively promoted Chinese policies and practices. They established Mandarin as the national language and prohibited the use of all other languages, such as Taiwanese (Lin, 2009; Sandel, 2003). A long-time proponent of Confucianism, Chiang Kai-Shek formed the Chinese Cultural Renaissance Commission in 1966. A few years later he issued guidelines for "eating, clothing, dwelling, walking, education, and entertainment" in order to create a Chinese version of modern life rooted in Confucian principles (Qiao & Ma, 1973). In 1967, the government implemented a policy of 9-year compulsory education. Textbooks and curricula were standardized across the nation to emphasize the teaching of Chinese traditions, values, and literature, which remained unchanged until 1990 (Su, 2006; Wachman, 1994). These moves by the KMT regime occurred in reaction to the Chinese Communist Party, which was anti-Confucian and which launched the Cultural Revolution in mainland China in 1966, and they helped to promote the legitimacy of the KMT's authority in Taiwan. The parents of the children in our study were growing up and attending school during this campaign to promote Confucian values.

In the second half of the 20th century, Taiwan achieved an "economic miracle," transforming an agrarian economy into an industrialized economy in a matter of decades. By the 1980s, Taiwan had become the world's 13th largest trading nation and the fifth largest trading partner of the United States (Cohen, 1988; Gold, 1986). By 1990, the average per capita income exceeded U.S.$8,000, and Taiwan had become a consumer society with a low unemployment rate, a relatively equitable income distribution, and a significant trade surplus (Simon & Kau, 1992). Economic development had its costs, however, including traffic jams, severe noise and air pollution, and increasing rates of violent crime (Simon & Kau, 1992).

Social change happened concurrently. In the 1990s, 40% of the nation's workforce had a high school diploma, the adult literacy rate was 92%, and a growing number of women entered the workforce (Cohen, 1988). Also, more women continued to work after their children were born. Although this meant that the need for child care was greater than ever, many young couples preferred to establish their own two-generation households, rather than live with the husband's parents in the traditional three-generation household in which grandmothers, mothers, and other female relatives shared domestic and child-care responsibilities.

In the political sphere, change was slower but no less dramatic. Martial law, in effect for 40 years, was lifted in 1987 (Simon & Kau, 1992), allowing Taiwanese residents to visit their mainland relatives for the first time. Shortly thereafter, political protests and opposition parties were legalized. The first direct presidential election was held in 1996, initiating a transition from the KMT's one-party dictatorship to a more democratic form of government.

As a result of migration from outlying areas, space was at a premium in Taipei, and nearly everyone lived in compact apartments. In contrast to American cities, residential segregation by social class was uncommon. Owing to rapid urban growth, pragmatic factors such as housing costs, access to good schools or convenient public transportation, or preference for new versus old buildings guided residential choices. A physician and a fruit vendor or a professor and a gas station attendant might live in the same apartment building. Most residents did not know their neighbors, and social networks were seldom formed on the basis of geographical proximity. Instead, precedence was given to extended family networks and, to a lesser extent, to social ties developed through schools and churches.

Unlike Taipei, Chicago is a mosaic of distinct neighborhoods. Longwood is a middle-class neighborhood that has had a strong Irish-American identity for nearly 100 years. Holidays such as St. Patrick's Day are enthusiastically observed and include an annual neighborhood parade. Civic organizations worked actively to preserve the special character and small-town ambience of this community, which is renowned locally for the beauty of its streets and houses, several of which are on the National Historic Registry. Many residents held the newly established shopping mall in contempt and worked actively to combat the homogenization they saw in nearby suburbs. At the same time, Longwood responded to demographic changes in the surrounding area, especially the expansion of a nearby African-American neighborhood. In the 1970s, Longwood resisted the trend toward "white flight" from the city and instead worked toward increasing ethnic integration. Although most families continued to praise the neighborhood and take tremendous pride in the stability of their community, several expressed concerns about its ability to sustain itself in the face of continuing diversification.

To the casual passerby, Longwood did not look or sound "urban." It was a neighborhood of large, single-family houses located on quiet, tree-lined streets. Built before World War II, the typical house had an expansive and well-manicured backyard. "For Sale" signs rarely appeared since property was sold by word of mouth. One community member explained that Longwood inhabitants expected residents to "keep up the neighborhood." If a new resident did not maintain his lawn to expected standards, neighbors would "drop by to see if everything was alright." Children often rode their bikes or tricycles on the sidewalks or played in their front yards.

Longwood's standing as a community derived not only from its physical location and neighborhood boundaries but also from its common cultural heritage and cohesive social network. Many adult residents had grown up in Longwood, and their parents and siblings still lived in the neighborhood. Many were actively involved in one of the local Catholic churches, and most sent their children to the Catholic school they themselves attended. Thus, Longwood families were bound by ties of culture, religion, family history, and active participation to a community that had a unique identity within the larger urban environment. Unlike Taipei, where the extended family seemed to be the most important unit of social organization beyond the immediate family, in Longwood the community, the church, and the extended family interlocked to provide young children with extensive contact with kin and nonkin.

Longwood's intergenerational stability may suggest that it had changed little from an earlier era. Certainly, the loyalty and "rootedness" that Longwood engendered in the late 20th century set it apart from other middle-class American communities in which geographic mobility was a fact of life. One father in our study declined a business promotion because it would have required his family to move, choosing instead to become a policeman. Yet parents were keenly aware of how family life had changed. Although they came from large families—some had eight or nine siblings—three children was the norm in the current generation.

THE FAMILIES' SOCIAL ADDRESSES

The study is based on longitudinal data from six Longwood and six Taipei families. The samples were similar in several demographic characteristics. All were two-parent families who owned their own homes and were financially secure. Most of the parents were college educated, and several held advanced degrees. The focal children were 2 years old when the study began and 4 years old when it ended. The samples were balanced by gender in both sites, and each child had at least one sibling. The Taipei and Longwood families differed in family composition and religion. In Longwood, mothers were the primary caregivers, and each family had three children; in Taipei each family had two children, and a female relative (mother, grandmother, or aunt) was the primary caregiver. The Longwood families were Catholic; the Taipei families varied in their religious orientations (described later). The Taipei families were relatively "Westernized." All had close relatives living in the United States or Canada, and in two families, a parent had received

18

graduate or professional education in Europe or the United States. None of the Longwood families had lived abroad.

PROCEDURES: A LONGITUDINAL STUDY IN THREE PHASES

The investigation unfolded in three phases: fieldwork, home observations, and interviews.

In the initial *fieldwork* phase, ethnographers were assigned to research sites where they shared both language (Mandarin Chinese or English) and cultural background with prospective participants. A Taiwanese researcher worked in Taipei, and a European-American researcher worked in Longwood. This strategy allowed each ethnographer to draw upon her linguistic and cultural knowledge to familiarize herself with the research site, to recruit participants, and to interact with families in an ecologically valid and culturally appropriate manner.

In both sites, attempts to recruit participants via letters or phone calls from lists provided by local institutions were unsuccessful; recruitment depended on building personal networks through face-to-face contact. In Taipei, the ethnographer cultivated contacts with the staff at a daycare center, a school, and a community health center, and they introduced her to eligible families. Mutual acquaintances introduced her to other prospective participants. In Longwood, the ethnographer's entry into the community was facilitated by an acquaintance whose aunt lived in the community and another acquaintance who had worked at a popular preschool. These individuals invited the ethnographer to community events and introduced her to their friends and acquaintances. She also recruited participants through a babysitting cooperative and an in-home daycare provider.

The ethnographers selected families who met several criteria: child's age (2 years), child was developing normally according to parents, number of siblings (at least one), socioeconomic status (owned own home, college educated), and feasibility of conducting the study (the family was not too busy to schedule observation sessions).

When discussing the goals of the study with parents, the ethnographers explained that they wanted to investigate how young children learn language and communicate with their families at home under everyday conditions. The consent form (translated into Chinese for the Taipei parents) reiterated this message. After the parents signed the consent form, the ethnographer made frequent home visits to get acquainted and establish a comfortable working relationship with parents and children before conducting the first observation session. The length of this get-acquainted period varied, sometimes lasting several months.

19

In the longitudinal *observation* phase, researchers made home observations of the children and their families at 6-month intervals (2, 6, 3, 0, 3, 6, and 4, 0). At each age, 4 hr of interactions were audio- and video-recorded for each focal child. The researchers usually conducted two 2-hr observations on successive days. Each of these 2-hr observations included continuous recording of ongoing interactions and domestic activities in the household. Recording occurred in the living area (living room, kitchen, or playroom), not in bedrooms. These procedures yielded 192 hr of recorded home observations, 16 hr per child.

The final phase involved *interviews* with the primary caregivers about their childrearing goals and practices and their beliefs about personal storytelling. The interviews were conducted last in order to avoid drawing undue attention to personal storytelling during the observations. The interviews are not analyzed here; see Fung (1999), Miller et al., (2001), and Mintz (1999).

Researcher's Role

The nature of the ethnographer's role is an important issue in the large and growing literature on ethnographic research with children and families (e.g., Briggs, 1970; Clark, 2003; Corsaro, 1985, 2003; Gaskins et al., 1992; Miller, Hengst, & Wang, 2003; Thorne, 1993; Wolf, 1992) just as it is in any ethnographic research (e.g., Duneier, 1999). As discussed in Chapter I, because the objective of ethnographic work is to represent people's meanings and practices on their own terms, ethnographers try to position themselves in the local scene in a manner that does not disrupt local ecologies and social routines.

In this respect, the ethnographers in this study had an advantage at the outset in that they spoke the local languages and could rely on their cultural intuitions. They drew upon this knowledge in meeting families, getting to know them, and devising appropriate roles for the observation sessions. It would not have been appropriate in either case to pretend to be an "invisible" observer, who declined to interact with child or other family members. Indeed, such a stance would have undermined the ecological and cultural validity of the observations. Thus, both ethnographers tried to behave like a family friend who had stopped by for a casual visit and to cultivate a comfortable relationship with the child and other family members. In addition, because the goal of the study was to understand how stories operate as a medium of children's everyday socialization, the researchers did not elicit stories from children or "push" narrative talk. Rather, their job was to participate in the local scene as best they could. If the focal child approached the ethnographer and launched into a story, she responded with interest; if a parent invited a story from the researcher, she obliged. In other words, like all ethnographers, the researchers were both "participants" and "observers" who tried to fashion for themselves culturally viable ways of interacting (see Miller, 1996, and Miller et al., 1996, for further discussion of the ethnographers' roles).

Transcription and Coding of Narratives

The first step in organizing the data involved viewing the videotapes to identify all stories of personal experience involving the child. This was done for each child at each age. These stories were then transcribed verbatim. The details of these procedures, including definitional criteria for identifying stories of personal experience, are described in Chapter III. Here we note several general features of our procedures. In keeping with the language socialization tradition, all transcription and coding of data were done in the relevant languages (Chinese or English).

The next step involved examining each corpus of stories to discern patterns of interpretation and enactment. The Taiwanese members of the research team worked with the Taipei corpus and the European-American members with the Longwood corpus. The goal was to understand each corpus on its own terms, rather than imposing one culture's patterns on the other. Again, this emic cultural analysis (also called derived or inductive categories) is standard practice in ethnographic research (Bloom, 1974; Hymes, 1996; Pike, 1967) and has been used increasingly by researchers studying development in cultural context (Corsaro, 2005; Duncan et al., 2007; Fung, 1999; Fung & Chen, 2001; Gaskins et al., 1992; Miller et al., 2003). For each analysis reported in the succeeding chapters, the Taiwanese and American researchers talked with one another about their data, discussing particular examples at length; eventually they came up with a set of common codes. This was a deeply intercultural process in which everyone involved became more aware of her taken-for-granted cultural biases and assumptions (see Schieffelin, 1990, and Wang, Wiley, & Zhou, 2007, for discussion of coding as an intercultural process). The codes were then applied to the stories, and intercoder reliability estimates were conducted.

FAMILY LIFE AND PARENTAL FOLK THEORIES IN TAIPEI AND LONGWOOD

Taipei

As members of the first "middle-class" generation in Taiwan (Hsiao, 1989), the Taipei parents enjoyed a high standard of living: good jobs, home ownership, discretionary income, and high hopes for the future of their children. Born in the 1950s and 1960s, they were raising their children in a world whose physical parameters had changed radically from their own childhood experience of one-story houses with yards. The ethnographer (Fung, 1994), who was of the same generation as the parents, remembered her childhood in Taipei, "The backyard of my parents' house was adjacent to rice fields. One of our neighbors raised pigs and another sold coal balls, made of coal dust and clay, which were the major source of fuel . . . . [The children] played in the streets, and in the fields where buffalo and chickens were familiar companions" (p. 72).

The children in our study inhabited a smaller, less green, and more vertical physical space. Built in the 1960s, most apartment buildings were four or five stories high, with an internal staircase. Although the families lived in different areas of the city, their apartments were similar in size (1,200 square feet) and floor plan. The living space was divided into a living room, dining room, small kitchen, three bedrooms, and one or two bathrooms. Housing accounted for the largest chunk of the family budget. One household included three generations; the others were nuclear family households. All of the families kept in close contact with extended family members, and some had daily access to grandparents.

The Taiwanese sample reflected the ethnic, linguistic, and religious diversity of their generation. The grandparents of the focal children included "mainlanders" (i.e., those who came to Taiwan from mainland China in the 1940s) as well as native-born Taiwanese. Although half the parents were fluent in Taiwanese, they preferred to speak Mandarin Chinese, the nation's official language, with their children. Many Taipei parents wanted their children to learn Mandarin as early as possible so that they would be prepared for school, where the language of instruction was Mandarin (Farris, 1988). Religion was another source of variability. Some families did not practice a religion. In other cases, folk religion wove through the families in complex and subtle ways, sometimes coexisting with other religious practices. For example, in one family the parents worshipped at folk temples, but the primary caregiver was a devout Protestant. In another family, the grandmother worshipped daily at a Protestant church yet remained strongly committed to folk religious beliefs.

Two of the mothers in the study were full-time housewives. In two additional cases, the mothers considered themselves to be full-time housewives but chose to send their children to nursery school for part of the day, beginning at 1 year of age; this was done when the second child was born or to allow the mother to frequent the stock market. In the fifth family the maternal grandmother lived in the household and took care of the children while the mother worked full-time as a university professor. In the sixth family the focal child and her sibling lived with their maternal aunt and her teenage children while the parents worked full-time in professional jobs in a distant part of the city; these children spent time with their parents only on weekends. By 3,6, all but one of the children attended half-day or full-day kindergarten or preschool. This practice supported Taiwanese parents' belief that providing a structured learning environment as early as possible would benefit their children.

The children's early years of life were spent in close physical and emotional proximity to their mother or other primary caregiver. She slept with the children to provide prompt care during the night. This practice did not reflect space constraints; each child had an individual bed in a room shared with a sibling. Except for excursions to the grocery store, visits with relatives in another part of the city, or trips to school to pick up an older sibling, the children spent most of their time at home. Their days were punctuated by meals and a long nap in the early afternoon. Caregivers talked to the children, pretended with them (Haight et al., 1999), helped them with puzzles, and played board or card games with them. When caregivers were busy, the youngsters played alone or with their sibling or watched television. In each family, the children had a modest number of toys, such as stuffed animals, blocks, and matchbox cars that filled a shelf or two in a closet or fit into a few toy boxes.

Children saw their fathers in the evenings and on the weekends. After the family dinner, fathers might play or watch television with the children, read them classical poems, or teach them Chinese characters. Bedtime for adults and children alike was usually 10:00 to 11:00 p.m. Weekends were a time for family activities, such as picnics in the public parks, visiting or dining out with grandparents and other relatives, or going to the flower market or a book exhibition.

The children's social life thus revolved around their immediate and extended family. Apart from siblings or cousins, these preschoolers had little peer experience prior to 3, 6. Since their families lived in buildings in which neighbors were unacquainted, the children kept to their own apartments. Only those who attended day care had regular contact with nonkin of their own age.

Caregivers held high standards for their children's conduct, a practice that is consistent with Confucian values. Wu (1996) argued that a key principle of Confucian parenting is that children be taught and disciplined as soon as they can talk and walk. We observed that children as young as 2 years old were expected to negotiate a home environment that was not child-proofed, offering the temptation of open cabinets and fragile objects. They were expected to listen attentively to their elders, comprehend what was said, and behave accordingly. Caregivers also corrected grammar and mispronunciations and rehearsed rhymes and poems. They made sure the children knew their full name, their parents' names, and their address and phone number. Literacy skills were actively cultivated. Parents read to their children and taught them to draw; some used flash cards to teach Chinese characters or numbers. The mothers reported that their children were toilet trained by 18 months, and several said that they had begun toilet training at 6 months. When the first author visited the families, she was astonished at the children's self-control. On her arrival, she gave each 2-year-old a wrapped present decorated with small candies, but, in keeping with proper etiquette, they waited until she had departed to open the gift.

In addition to setting high standards for their youngsters' behavior, the parents in our study embraced the Confucian idea that shame is a virtue. Heidi Fung's work (Fung, 1999, 2006; Fung & Chen, 2001) demonstrates that the parents routinely engaged in shaming as a complex, nuanced disciplinary practice. They felt obligated to deal with the child's misdeeds promptly and to rehearse and reenact the rules of conduct with the child from time to time. Young children's transgressions were often construed as opportunities to situate the rules concretely in their immediate experience. The parents might bring the lesson to its fullest effect by invoking shameful feelings in the child via a configuration of assorted markers and communicative channels. Most of these seemingly harmful practices were done in a playful manner with an attempt to cultivate a sense of discretion-shame (*chi*) in the child who should be responsible for her own behavior and strive to improve. In doing so, the parents tried to protect the child from unnecessary disgrace-shame (*xiu*) caused by her further transgression.

Still another Confucian value—appreciation of didactic narrative—was evident in mothers' folk theories of personal narrative, as revealed in interviews (Miller et al., 2001). Although the Taipei mothers showed little awareness of the narrative practices that we observed (see Chapters III–V), they strongly endorsed the related practice of *parents* telling stories of personal experience *to* their children. They reported hearing such stories from their parents when they were young and said that they engaged in the same practice with their own children. In the examples that they cited, parents were consistently portrayed as worthy of emulation (Miller et al., 2001). Often there was also an implied criticism of the child. These pairings—the admirable parent and the fallible child—seemed intended to motivate the child to do better by following the parental example. They also indexed an asymmetry between parents and children of the sort that Hsu (1971, 1983) has argued is characteristic of Chinese families as well as the high value placed on deliberate moral instruction (e.g., Chao, 1994; Chu, 1972; Ho, 1986; Wu, 1981, 1996).

Longwood

Although houses in Longwood varied in style and floor plan, each was spacious enough—two stories, four bedrooms, two bathrooms—to easily accommodate several children. One family lived in the same house in which the mother had grown up. The homes' interiors reflected an emphasis on family life, containing playrooms or recreation rooms filled with toys. Designating

24

specific portions of a home as children's or family space was not meant to restrict children, however. Instead, it signaled the high priority that families placed on attending to their young. In short, family and community life was very child-centered and consciously designed to provide an "optimal" environment for children. At the same time, each member of the family, including the youngest, had his or her own space and property. Children either had their own bedrooms or shared a bedroom with a same-sex sibling.

None of the Longwood mothers worked full-time outside the home, believing that very young children should be cared for by their mothers. However, they had worked as social workers, clerks, or teachers before having children and expected to return to work once the children were older. Several mothers also noted that they chose to stay home with their preschoolers because they did not want to miss the opportunity to observe and influence their children's development. Some mothers participated in "babysitting coops," which allowed them to share child care, and a few provided day cares in their homes.

Thus, very young children spent the majority of their time at home under the supervision of their mothers. While children played with siblings or peers or watched television or videos, mothers often took care of household chores, periodically checking on the children. They also joined in children's play or read books to them. The mothers varied in the degree to which they provided structured activities such as baking, doing a craft project, or having the child help with the laundry, but all allowed their children plenty of time for creative, self-initiated play (Haight et al., 1999). The children's days were organized around meals, an afternoon nap, and often an outing (e.g., shopping, watching an older sibling's softball game, a trip to a park or a museum, a visit to a nearby relative's home). By 3,0, several of the children began to spend a few half-days per week at one of the local nursery schools, two of which were church affiliated.

Fathers spent time with their children in the evenings and on weekends. Many Longwood fathers also moonlighted as baseball and soccer coaches for local children's teams. Fathers interacted with preschoolers at dinner and afterwards by reading, playing, or watching videos with them. Fathers also helped with bath and bedtime. Most preschoolers were put to bed between 8:00 and 9:00 p.m.; older children enjoyed the privilege of a later bedtime.

In contrast to the Taiwanese youngsters, young children in Longwood experienced a world that was heavily populated with other children both inside and outside the home (Mintz, 1999). In addition to siblings and cousins, children made friends with their neighbors on the block. In several homes, children ran in and out of each other's houses and yards on a casual and frequent basis. Preplanned play dates, birthday and other holiday parties, and visits to local parks provided other forums for children to meet and

25

interact. Thus, early in their lives, Longwood children were introduced to a peer-based social life.

Within this highly social environment Longwood youngsters were exposed to a great deal of talk. As in the "mainstream" American cultural case described by Ochs and Schieffelin (1984), mothers talked directly to their youngsters, taking into account the child's perspective and language level but building on and expanding the child's semantic intent. This tendency to adapt to the child was evident in a variety of other practices as well, including childproofing the environment, use of child-scaled objects and furniture, and abundant provision of toys. Talking and listening to children, reading to them, pretending with them, or teaching them to play baseball were not just enjoyable experiences but ways in which parents could provide the kind of focused attention that they believed promoted healthy development (Mintz, 1999).

Several mothers expressed the view that children need a great deal of adult attention to feel happy and good about themselves (Mintz, 1999). In discussing a popular preschool teacher, they spoke admiringly of her ability to foster children's self-esteem. Indeed, interviews with the Longwood mothers revealed that promoting children's self-esteem was a matter of the first importance to them (Mintz, 1999). They believed that self-esteem provides the foundation for happiness, inner strength, and moral autonomy and spoke of the devastating consequences of low self-esteem for children's psychological functioning and success in the world. Some mothers invoked self-esteem when discussing how their approach to childrearing differed from their parents'.

Self-esteem also came into play in Longwood mothers' ethnotheories about personal storytelling (Miller et al., 2001). Like their Taipei counterparts, they showed little awareness of the practice we observed, namely telling stories of their young children's past experience (see Chapters III–V) but spoke favorably and at length about the related practice of telling stories about their *own* experience *to* their children. However, unlike the Taipei mothers, the Longwood mothers did not narrate their own admirable deeds to their children. Rather, they cited narrative examples in which they narrated their faults and shortcomings as a way of conveying that they too were fallible as children (Miller et al., 2001). One mother said that she used such stories as a way to "reassure them [her children] ... that something they did wasn't really that bad" (p. 172). This pattern implies a desire to protect the child's psychological well-being and to reduce the asymmetry in the parent–child relationship. Miller et al. (2001) concluded, "Longwood mothers seem more worried about undermining children's psychological health and remaining approachable to them than about undermining their own authority" (p. 178).

And yet, Longwood parents did expect preschoolers to behave well. When children misbehaved in minor ways, such as refusing to share with a playmate, quarreling with a sibling, or hanging on the dining room curtains, parents intervened promptly and repeatedly if necessary. At the same time, most parents expressed an understanding of young children's willfulness and appreciated the clever ways their youngsters attempted to get what they wanted. When a serious behavior problem occurred, such as hitting or biting another person or an uncontrollable temper tantrum, parents resorted to "time out" or revoked a privilege or treat (Mintz, 1999). When misdeeds were discussed, emphasis was placed on the rationale for the rule and on helping the child understand why it was important to comply. But concern with the child's self-esteem impinged here as well. Mothers said that they drew a distinction between "being bad" and "doing bad things" (Miller et al., 2001; Mintz, 1999). By explaining to the child that his action was bad but that he was not, they attempted to correct the child without harming his self-esteem.

In sum, the children whom we studied in the late 1980s and early 1990s were not "typical" Taiwanese or "typical" Americans. They were growing up in families who occupied a relatively privileged position within their respective societies. Their parents—the first middle-class Taiwanese, on the one hand, and heirs to a cohesive Irish–Catholic neighborhood, on the other—created a particular cultural idiom at a particular moment in history. Despite recent changes in the immediate community and the surrounding area, Longwood residents preserved their identity and continuity with the past. Families took pride in their family values and child-centered way of life, rooted in long-term prosperity. Yet they chose to break with the tradition of having very large families. Mothers said they were raising their children differently than they had been raised and voiced a strong desire to foster their children's self-esteem. In Taipei, the balance between change and continuity leaned in the other direction. The Taiwanese children inhabited a world that differed radically from the world in which their parents and grandparents grew up. We entered their lives at a time when the symptoms of modernization were blindingly obvious. Yet, as the succeeding chapters will show, traditional Confucian values were still powerfully alive in the mundane practice of personal storytelling.

III. INTERPRETIVE FRAMEWORKS IN ROUTINE PRACTICES

Eva Chian-Hui Chen, Peggy J. Miller, Heidi Fung, and Benjamin R. Boldt

As described in the previous chapter, the Taipei and Longwood children were 2,6 when we made the first recorded observations. At this age, personal storytelling occurred frequently as part of everyday family life in both sites, but one interpretive lens was more salient in the Taipei stories and another in the Longwood stories (Miller et al., 1996, 1997). In this chapter, we track the same families longitudinally, asking questions that follow directly from these findings: Did personal storytelling continue to occur routinely in the Taipei and Longwood families as the children got older? And did the participants continue to privilege culture-specific interpretive frameworks when narrating children's past experiences? Specifically, did the Taipei families continue to slant their personal storytelling in a didactic direction, while the Longwood families continued to slant theirs in a child-affirming direction? As outlined in Chapter I, we expected that personal storytelling would remain a robust practice during the preschool years and that it would continue to embody these contrasting frameworks. This chapter also extends our previous work conceptually by offering a more comprehensive coding of the child-affirming framework.

The chapter unfolds as follows: We begin with the routine nature of personal storytelling, followed by the privileging of the didactic framework in Taipei, and then, the privileging of the child-affirming framework in Longwood. The next section brings the differences between the didactic and child-affirming frameworks into sharper focus by comparing two stories of babyish behavior, one from Taipei and one from Longwood. The chapter concludes with a discussion.

DID PERSONAL STORYTELLING OCCUR ROUTINELY?

Identification and Transcription of Narrations

A total of 144 hr of recorded interactions in the Taipei and Longwood families were analyzed, building on the earlier analysis of 48 hr at 2,6, for a total sample of 192 hr of recorded interactions. The initial step in processing the data involved extracting the spontaneously occurring stories of personal experience. These stories were identified according to the coding criteria established and reliably applied in Miller et al. (1997). A narration of personal experience was defined as an event involving the child and one or more other persons in which the child's past experience was related in temporal order. A narration of personal experience invoked a nonimmediate past event (i.e., a particular event that occurred prior to the taping sessions) or a class of past events (i.e., an event that occurred routinely prior to the taping sessions) in which the child was portrayed as a protagonist. The narration began with the first utterance that referred to the past event and ended with the final utterance that referred to the past event.

In the following example, Longlong was playing with a balloon when his mother prompted him to talk about an event that occurred the day before. After her initial prompt, child and mother took turns relating what happened, representing the events as unfolding in temporal sequence: Longlong went to the doctor, and the doctor gave him a sticker and a balloon, the very balloon that triggered his mother's prompt.

Example 1: Longlong (2,6) a narration of personal experience

Mother:	**Longlong, you, you tell auntie [Researcher], yesterday (pause) where did you go? [First utterance]**
Child:	To call the doctor.
Mother:	To see the doctor.
Child:	To see the doctor.
Mother:	To see, to see the doctor, didn't you?
Child:	Yes. (Pause) To see the doctor.
Mother:	What did the doctor give you?
Child:	Give [me] stickers.
Mother:	What did [he] give you?
Child:	Give [me] stickers.
Mother:	Balloon.
Child:	Balloon.
Mother:	**Who gave you that balloon? [Final utterance]**
Child:	(Says nothing, looks downward, and resumes playing with the balloon.)

This story ended when Longlong shifted his attention away from the conversation about his past experience and resumed playing with the balloon, and his mother did not pursue the topic. Thus, the final utterance was his mother's question, "Who gave you that balloon?" Although this narration is very simple, involving brief contributions by Longlong, it meets the criteria for

29

a story of past experience and exemplifies the baseline for our longitudinal analyses.

In order to establish intercoder reliability estimates for the identification of narrations, we randomly chose four 30-min segments of video-recorded family interactions at each site at each age. Two independent coders viewed and coded these interactions. First, the coder identified every narration. The proportions of agreement for the Taipei sample ranged from 0.90 to 1.00, with a mean of 0.94; the analogous figures for Longwood were 0.85 to 1.00, with a mean of 0.95. Second, each coder identified the initial and final utterance of each story. The figures for Taipei ranged from 0.81 to 0.96 with a mean of 0.90; for Longwood from 0.81 to 0.92, with a mean of 0.86. Disagreements were resolved through discussion.

Narrations were transcribed verbatim by native speakers of English or Mandarin, following the standards of CHILDES (Child Language Data Exchange System, MacWhinney, 1991), and each transcript was checked for accuracy by a second native speaker. We then tallied the number of narrations that occurred at each age in each site and determined the length of narrations by tallying the number of utterances per narration. We also computed the mean and median frequency of narrations, the mean and median rate per hour, and the mean length of narrations in each site.

Results: Frequency of Narrations

The frequencies and rates of narrations per hour are displayed in Table 1. In order to make it easier for readers to follow the developmental sequences across the entire age range, here and elsewhere in this chapter we include findings from the 2,6 data point, presented originally in Miller et al. (1997), along with the new results at the later ages. Overall, summing across the four ages, Taipei and Longwood families produced remarkably similar numbers of narrations (Taipei: 470 vs. Longwood: 420), for a total corpus of 890 narrations. In addition, narrations occurred at stable rates in both Taipei and Longwood, whether one considers mean or median rates per hour, although there was some fluctuation at the later ages. In Taipei, stories occurred at mean rates of 3.8 to 5.8 across the age points; in Longwood, the mean rates ranged from 3.6 to 4.7.

Table 2 displays the frequencies and rates of narrations in a different way, focusing on variation within each group. This table reveals similarity between the Taipei and Longwood groups in the amount of individual variation.

The overall and mean lengths of narrations are also displayed in Table 2. Summing across the four ages, the 890 narrations yielded a total of 14,398 utterances. Looking comparatively and summing across ages, the Taipei and

TABLE 1

NARRATIONS OF PERSONAL EXPERIENCE ACROSS AGES: FREQUENCIES AND RATES/HOUR
(TAIPEI/LONGWOOD)

| Age | Overall | Frequency | | Rate/Hour | |
		Mean	Median	Mean	Median
2,6	92/112	15.3/18.7	15.5/16.0	3.8/4.7	3.9/4.0
3,0	132/109	22.0/18.2	18.0/19.5	5.5/4.6	4.5/4.9
3,6	107/113	17.8/18.8	18.5/16.5	4.5/4.7	4.6/4.1
4,0	139/86	23.2/14.2	22.5/12.0	5.8/3.6	5.6/3.0
Total	470/420	19.6/17.5	18.3/16.3	4.9/4.4	4.6/4.1

TABLE 2

NARRATIONS OF PERSONAL EXPERIENCE ACROSS AGES: VARIATION WITHIN GROUPS
(TAIPEI/LONGWOOD)

Age	Frequency	Rate/Hour	Length (utterances)	Mean/Narration
2,6	6–25/10–39	1.50–6.25/2.50–9.75	1,116/1,811	12.1/16.2
3,0	12–35/7–29	3.00–8.75/1.75–7.25	2,313/1,468	17.5/13.5
3,6	8–33/14–28	2.00–8.25/3.50–7.00	1,694/1,702	15.8/15.1
4,0	20–28/10–25	5.00–7.00/2.50–6.25	2,326/1,968	16.7/22.9
Total	–	–	7,449/6,949	15.8/16.6

Longwood families produced stories of similar length. The trends with respect to age were not consistent. For the Taipei families story length increased from 2,6 to 3,0 and then fluctuated. For the Longwood families story length was stable until 4,0 when it increased; at this age, they produced a relatively small number of relatively long stories.

These findings suggest that youngsters from Taipei and Longwood encountered a great many stories about their past experiences during the preschool years. In addition, as was the case at 2,6, the expanded corpus encompassed a great variety of content in both sites. For example, events involving physical harm to the child were narrated in Longwood (e.g., the child incurred small injuries or "boo-boos," fell against the coffee table and hurt his chin, suffered a severe asthma attack, got stung by a bee) and in Taipei (e.g., the child fell off the bed, got a bruise when playing on the slide in the park, cut her finger, fell while taking a shower, got scratched by a monkey when feeding it at the zoo). Stories of enjoyable family events were also narrated in both sites: Longwood families narrated Thanksgiving, Christmas, and Easter get-togethers; birthday parties; a communion party; sports events; visits to museums and zoos; and a trip to Colorado. Taipei families narrated Chinese New Year celebrations, family dinners, birthday parties, visits to zoos and libraries, a trip to Japan, a firework display, and visits to grandparents' homes. Still other stories focused on events that were simply interesting or unusual (e.g., in Longwood: playing a new board game, watching a polar bear blow bubbles or a friend do magic tricks, seeing an ultrasound photo of the baby in mom's belly and thinking that it looked like a monkey; in Taipei: sending the family dog to a doggy hotel when the family was traveling, making an audio tape and sending greetings to grandparents overseas, seeing a mouse running in the kitchen and catching it with mommy, performing on the stage on Children's Day, picking up daddy at the airport, visiting a newborn baby in the hospital).

In the remainder of this chapter, we examine the entire corpus from each site to determine which of the stories embodied the culturally salient interpretive frameworks that emerged in our earlier work. Given the variety of events that can be cast in narrative form and the multiplicity of frameworks available in any culture (Briggs, 1998; Lutz & White, 1986), we would not expect the didactic framework to apply to every story in the Taipei corpus, nor the child-affirming framework to every story in the Longwood samples. We looked instead for comparative differences in the frequency with which these different frameworks were enacted and in corresponding qualitative differences in patterns of interpretation based on microlevel analysis.

DID TAIPEI FAMILIES CONTINUE TO PRIVILEGE A DIDACTIC FRAMEWORK?

To answer this question, we applied the didactic coding scheme developed by Miller et al. (1997) when the children were 2,6 to the stories that occurred at 3,0, 3,6, and 4,0. That is, we analyzed the content (narrated transgressions), function (occasioning transgressions), and structure (endings) of identified personal narrations.

Didactic Codes Defined

Narrated Transgressions

This code was applied to the story if the child was portrayed as violating a social or moral rule in the past, as interpreted from the perspective of at least one of the narrating participants. For example, a narrator recounted the child's fight with friends on an earlier occasion. If the narrator commented that the child was being rude, then the narration was coded as a narrated transgression. If, however, the narrator indicated that the child was brave in standing up for himself or herself, then the narration was not coded as a narrated transgression. Narrated transgressions were identified on the basis of the following kinds of specific evidence: (a) explicit evaluation of the child's past act. For instance, Angu's (3,6) cousin initiated a story by saying *"Shame* on you, you were so *stupid*!" in reference to the previous day, when she and Angu were walking along the street, and Angu accidentally fell down, dropped one of her shoes into the gutter, and started to cry. Steve (3,6) said, "Mommy got *mad* at me," referring to a past experience when he misbehaved and was given a time out. (b) Implicit evaluation of the child's past act, as indicated by intonation, stress, and/or implicit characterizations. Jingjing's (4,0) mother asked her, in a *disapproving* tone, "Jingjing, why did you do that? There was someone saying dirty words on the bus, and you followed that person and repeated the dirty words!" Karen's (3,6) father remarked, in a *disapproving* voice, "Glad you weren't here yesterday. She got into Diane's makeup and she came in looking like someone had hit her in the head, in the face with a baseball bat (gestures with his hand over his eye). She got all purple, and it looked like she got a shiner." (c) Explicit reference to the violated rule in the past event. Longlong's (3,0) mother announced, *"Only girls wear lipstick. Boys do not wear lipstick,"* referring to Longlong's act of picking up a lipstick and asking his mother to put makeup on him. Tommy's (3,6) older brother recounted how Tommy had behaved badly at the babysitter's house and then said, "Um, so I told my babysitter and my babysitter said, *'Tommy, we don't jump on furniture.'"*

As we analyzed the narrated transgressions, it became apparent that as the children grew older, they became more aware of the implications of their own past experiences and were more capable of preventing themselves from violating rules. This never happened when the children were 2,6. We therefore decided to extend the definition of narrated transgression to include narrations in which the child indicated that he or she *did not* commit a transgression. For example, when Yoyo's (3,6) mother related that the family dog was punished because it scratched and tore a hole in the screen door, Yoyo responded, "I *did not,* I *did not* scratch it, because I am not a dog." Similarly, while playing with his brother, Yoyo (4,0) asserted, "We *did not* fight with each other this morning."

Occasioning Transgressions

Unlike the narrated transgression code that concerned the child's behaviors in the past, the occasioning transgression code concerned the child's behaviors in the here-and-now moment of the observation. Our purpose in applying this code was to investigate whether the child's present transgression served as a prompt for the narration of the child's past transgression. Again, only transgressions that were interpreted as such by at least one of the participants were coded as occasioning transgressions. For example, while Didi (4,0) was playing by himself at home, he put his fingers into his mouth, which his mother interpreted as unsafe. She insisted that he take his fingers out of his mouth and then connected his current safety-related rule violation to a similar transgression that he had committed a few days earlier. In the earlier transgression, Didi failed to listen to his mother's admonition to stop jumping on the bed and ending up hitting his head on the window. Thus, Didi's mother treated her son's here-and-now transgression as an opportunity to remind him of a previous similar transgression that resulted in harm to himself. Similarly, when Amy (3,6) held a penny in her hand, an activity that her mother perceived as a transgression, she said to Amy, "You know what, honey, I don't want you to swallow that, so could you just throw that in the garbage please?" When Amy answered, "I won't," her mother insisted, "Throw it in the garbage, please." Then she added the following reminder about a previous occasion on which Amy committed a similar misdeed, "Well, you thought you wouldn't swallow that penny. Remember when you swallowed that penny in the summer and we had to take you to the hospital?"

The analysis of occasioning transgressions involved two steps. First, each narration coded as a *narrated* transgression was examined to determine whether it occurred immediately after an *occasioning* transgression, and then the proportion of narrated transgressions preceded by an occasioning transgression was computed. Second, in each research site at each age, 36 randomly selected narrations that did not invoke a past transgression were examined to determine whether they were occasioned by an immediately preceding transgression in the here-and-now. The proportion of these narrations was computed for each cultural setting.

Endings

Story endings were classified into three categories: didactic coda, attribute of the child, and new topic. A *didactic coda* referred to one or more statements made after the final utterance of the past event to bring the story back into the time frame of the present or future. Topic continuity was preserved, but there was a shift in temporal reference. In addition, a didactic coda extended the implication of the narration for the present or future in a way that invoked moral or social rules. For example, after telling a story about how Angu (4,0) did not want her mother to hold her hand when they went mountain climbing and thus ended up falling down and getting hurt, Angu's aunt wrapped up the narration by asking Angu, "Next time, will you push your mother away again?" An *attribute of the child* was applied if the story concluded with one or more utterances that mentioned a particular characteristic of the child. Like the didactic coda, this was likely to involve a temporal adverb or (in English) a tense shift to the present, future, or timeless frame but also involved an enduring quality that was exemplified in the narrated event. For instance, Longlong's (4,0) mother related that Longlong got upset and yelled at her when she shared his candies with other children. She ended the narration by saying, "You are so *stingy*. People won't treat you to candies in the future." Patrick's (3,6) mother related that he took all his asthma medication. She said, "Patrick is a very *brave* little boy though." Stories that ended with a shift of topic were coded as *new topic*. For example, Yoyo (3,6) and his brother co-narrated their performance in church on Christmas Eve. The story ended when Yoyo stood up, grabbed a toy bear, and walked into his bedroom. When Karen (4,0) and her father were co-narrating a trip to the movie theater, he asked Karen, "Who went, who went with us?" Rather than responding to her father's question, Karen asked him to give her a plate for her food, thereby shifting the topic from the story to the here-and-now activity of eating lunch.

We used the following procedures to obtain intercoder reliability estimates for the didactic codes (and for the child-affirming codes, presented later): in each cultural case at each age, at least .25 of all stories were coded by two independent coders, and proportions of agreement were calculated. Disagreements were resolved through discussion. Figures ranged from 0.86 to 0.97 with a mean of 0.94 (Taipei) and from 0.94 to 1.00 with a mean of 0.97 (Longwood) for narrated transgressions, from 0.89 to 1.00 with a mean of 0.97 (Taipei) and from 1.00 to 1.00 (Longwood) for occasioning transgressions, and from 0.89 to 0.96 with a mean of 0.93 (Taipei) and from 0.90 to 1.00 with mean of 0.95 (Longwood) for endings.

Results: Didactic Interpretive Framework

Narrated Transgressions

As shown in Table 3, the Longwood families produced only 21 stories in which the child's past transgressions were narrated. Moreover, the low frequency of narrated transgressions occurred at every age, ranging from 0.03 to 0.07, with an overall average of 0.05. By contrast, transgression stories accounted for 0.33 of the Taipei stories, with a range from 0.29 to 0.36 across the age points. That is, the proportional frequencies reveal that the Taipei families produced at least five times more narrated transgressions than their Longwood counterparts at every age. The median proportions showed a similar pattern of contrast between the two cultural groups. Thus, the striking disparity in the proportion of narrated transgressions that occurred at 2,6 (Miller et al., 1997) continued at 3,0, 3,6, and 4,0.

In the Taipei families, narrated transgressions included violations of general moral rules, such as telling lies, not listening to parents, and falsely accusing others (usually siblings) for one's own wrongdoing. Transgressions also included inappropriate emotional displays (e.g., crying, losing one's temper), engaging in unhealthy or unsafe behavior (e.g., eating too much candy, jumping on the bed), insensitivity to another's needs (e.g., trying to play with

TABLE 3

FREQUENCY AND PROPORTION OF NARRATED TRANSGRESSIONS AND OCCASIONING
TRANSGRESSIONS (TAIPEI/LONGWOOD)

	Narrated Transgressions		Occasioning Transgressions	
Age	Frequency	Proportion	Frequency	Proportion
2,6	32/8	.35/.07	16/1	.50/.13
3,0	46/3	.35/.03	8/1	.17/.50
3,6	38/6	.36/.05	7/1	.18/.14
4,0	40/4	.29/.05	14/0	.35/.00
Total	156/21	.33/.05	45/3	.29/.14

the baby when he was sleeping, disturbing classmates by playing too loudly, phoning father at whim without considering that he might be busy at work), inappropriate behaviors in public (e.g., fighting with classmates in school, making a lot of noise in the public library), disrespecting another's property (e.g., playing on the computer in father's office without asking permission), violating the rules of politeness (e.g., bad table manners), behaving in a greedy or self-indulgent manner (e.g., asking for new toys every time the family went shopping), and behaving carelessly and irresponsibly (e.g., not taking good care of personal belongings, causing food to be spilled).

Among the small number of narrated transgressions that occurred in Longwood, there was some similarity in the type of transgression, including violations of general moral rules (e.g., telling lies and falsely accusing others for one's own wrongdoing), engaging in unhealthy or unsafe behavior (e.g., putting a penny in one's mouth, hanging on pipes in the basement), inappropriate emotional displays (e.g., crying and whining), and disrespecting another's property (e.g., making a mess with water, pulling down the curtains, getting into mother's makeup).

However, the discrepancy between the Taipei and Longwood transgression stories extended beyond the difference in frequency to the manner in which children's past misdeeds were narrated. The Taipei families used shaming, power assertion, love withdrawal, and other "aggravating" strategies to convey the seriousness of the children's misdeeds. For example, after rebuking Didi (3,0) and his older sister for fighting over colored markers, their mother told the following story, "The other day, their father was really mad at them [for fighting]. He shouted at them and asked them to pack their stuff and leave the house." She then turned to Didi and his older sister and said, "Get out of the house! See who wants you? [We'll] give you to whomever, we don't want you." Not only did she relate that her husband had threatened to cast out the children on the earlier occasion, but she also used the same strategy when recounting their wrongdoing in the here-and-now. This example also illustrates another common feature of the Taipei stories, namely the repetition within a single story of threats of abandonment, strong rebukes, and/or shaming.

The Longwood families did not use such unmitigated strategies. On the rare occasion that they narrated their children's past transgressions, they downplayed the seriousness of the misdeeds, just as they had when the children were younger (Miller et al., 1997). For example, Patrick (2,6) and his brother told a story about a time when they were punished for being bad boys. However, neither they nor their mother could recall what the boys had done wrong. During the narration, the mother asked in mock surprise, "My kids being bad?" The entire narration was keyed playfully and ended with laughter (Miller et al., 1996).

In a similar example, Steve's (3,6) mother prompted him to narrate a past event in which he was disciplined.

Example 2: Steve (3,6) was given a time-out

Mother:	And what happened to Steve?
Child:	Mommy got mad at me (unintelligible).
Mother:	What happened?
Child:	(Unintelligible) Sit on the stairs.
Mother:	You had to sit on the stairs for five minutes, didn't you?
Researcher:	Oh, you had a time out?
Mother:	Uh hum, I love you.
Child:	(Turns away and then plays with his toys)

Although Steve and his mother related that she got mad at him and gave him a time out, here again the misdeed was omitted. Moreover, Steve's mother quickly reassured him with an explicit avowal of love. By pairing a past disciplinary event with an expression of love, Steve's mother enacted a variant of the "I love you but I don't like what you did" strategy that the Longwood mothers endorsed (Miller et al., 2001; Mintz, 1999). In interviews, they expressed the belief that in order to support children's self-esteem, it is important when disciplining children to remind them that they are loved despite their wrongdoing. This finding also emerged in another sample of middle-class European-American mothers in the Midwest (Miller et al., 2002).

Another strategy that was used only among the Longwood families was to put a positive spin on the misdeed. For example, in a story about a past event in which Patrick (4,0) engaged in the forbidden and dangerous act of hanging from the basement pipes, his mother added, "He's older now, he knows better . . . He was probably just a kid then, right, Patrick?" Instead of treating his past misdeed as a chance for reflection and remediation, Patrick's mother recast his misbehavior as something he had already outgrown. In a similar situation, a Taipei parent likely would have focused the child's attention on the wrongdoing, ensuring that he understood how he had gone astray and drawing out the implications for his future conduct.

Occasioning Transgressions

As can be seen in Table 3, narrated transgressions were rarely occasioned by a here-and-now transgression in the Longwood families. But in the Taipei families, 45 of 156 (0.29) narrated transgressions were preceded by here-and-now transgressions. The rates of occasioning transgressions fluctuated, showing no apparent pattern across the age range. Meimei (3,0) and her mother provided a good example of how a narrated transgression emerged from a here-and-now misdeed. The Taiwanese parents considered it to be impolite for a person who has received a gift from a guest to unwrap the gift in the guest's presence. Thus, when Meimei began to unwrap a birthday gift that the researcher had just given her, her mother stopped her immediately and told the researcher a story about a similar misdeed that Meimei had committed previously. "It happened to the birthday cake, too. [After we bought the cake] I put it in the car, but [when we arrived home] she couldn't wait for me to get out of the car. She was in such a hurry and [she grabbed the cake and] ran with the cake swinging in her hands. When we got into the house, the cake was a mess." Meimei's temptation to unwrap her birthday gift during the taping session served as an excellent opportunity for her mother to link Meimei's current misdeed to a past transgression, in which Meimei could not resist temptation.

Our second analysis revealed that nontransgression stories were not preceded by here-and-now transgressions in either cultural group.

Endings

As displayed in Table 4, adding a didactic coda to the end of a narration occurred infrequently in Taipei ($M = 0.06$, $N = 27$) but more frequently than in Longwood, where they were virtually nonexistent. Taken as a whole, the codas added 354 utterances to the Taipei corpus. Codas ranged from a brief comment to a lengthy discussion of the violated rule and the implications of not abiding by rules. Examples of brief codas included, "Being tricky is bad!"; "Don't keep opening and closing [the door of] your toy car; otherwise, what will happen?"; "Your brother then won't get angry, right? Tell me. (Pause) After you play with the clay, and then you clean it up, then your brother won't get angry at you."; "You are lying? Won't you be afraid of being punished by God? [God will] smack your bottom! Because Mimi [the family dog] is now in heaven."; and "Will you dare to play with the cable car again?"

TABLE 4

FREQUENCY AND PROPORTION OF STORY ENDINGS (TAIPEI/LONGWOOD)

Age	Didactic Coda		Attribute of the Child		New Topic	
	Frequency	Proportion	Frequency	Proportion	Frequency	Proportion
2,6	8/0	.09/.00	22/7	.24/.06	62/105	.67/.94
3,0	7/0	.05/.00	16/1	.12/.01	109/108	.83/.99
3,6	8/1	.08/.01	11/7	.10/.06	88/105	.82/.93
4,0	4/2	.03/.02	12/3	.09/.03	123/81	.88/.94
Total	27/3	.06/.01	61/18	.13/.04	382/399	.81/.95

An example of a narration that ended with a lengthy didactic coda involved Didi (4,0). His mother and older sister told a story about an incident in which Didi got lost at a night market, terrifying his parents. Didi's mother explained the implications of his serious misbehavior in a didactic coda that was longer than the narrated event itself. She first reminded Didi of how dangerous it could be for him to stray from his parents when they go out in public. She then went on to explain the importance of listening to parents and teachers, lest one end up in big trouble.

Example 3: Didi (4,0) a long didactic coda

Mother:	That was because you met a good person. If it were a bad person [who had found you when you were lost], he would have cut off your hands, legs, and even tongue! It would be a misfortune. Right or (interrupted)?
Child:	Right. Mommy (interrupted) (stands up from the floor)
Mother:	Therefore, Daddy and Mommy are trying hard to take care of you two. Why (interrupted)
Child:	(Approaches Mother and says loudly) Mommy would get very sad.
Mother:	Right. Then you, why do you never follow Mommy closely? You never do that when [we] take you out.
Child:	(Goes back to his drawing on the floor)
Sister:	I didn't do that.
Mother:	Yes, it is very dangerous once you get lost. Therefore, that's the reason why Daddy and Mommy take care of you, right? You need to be, be taken care of by Daddy and Mommy. And you need to listen to whatever Daddy and Mommy have told you. You are still young, you don't understand.
Sister:	What does it mean "don't understand"?

Mother:	[To Sister] It means there are still a lot of things you don't know. Don't the teachers, don't you go to school, and the teachers teach you, then you learn, learn something (interrupted)
Child:	(Sits straight and then points to his drawing) Look, they are playing. (Lies on his back on the floor and draws again)
Mother:	Isn't it right? There are a lot of things. Our world is so huge, and there are a lot of things going on. So, "a lot of things [you need to learn]" means [you] don't understand. "Don't understand" means (loudly) you don't know!
Child:	Don't know (unintelligible).
Mother:	You don't know, and therefore Daddy and Mommy are going to teach you, and you should listen carefully when we teach you. When the teachers teach you, listen carefully. When the teachers teach you, it doesn't mean you can talk to other classmates. If you don't pay attention in class, I think you are going to have big troubles!

In this didactic coda, Didi's mother used a number of emotionally charged strategies to persuade her son and daughter to take her admonitions to heart. First, she used fear induction to communicate the awful consequences that could have happened as a result of Didi's misbehavior: "If it were a bad person [who had found you when you were lost], he would have cut off your hands, legs, and even tongue! It would be a misfortune!" Interrupting his mother's explanation, Didi responded, "Mommy would get very sad," indicating that he understood the emotional impact that such a misfortune would have on his mother. His mother went on to articulate the larger goal that motivated his parents' actions, namely their desire to take care of him and his sister and to protect them from the dangers of the world, dangers that they were too young to understand. This is why, she continued, Didi and his sister need to listen to their parents. In response to Didi's sister's query, the mother repeated her reasoning, explaining again why it is so important for parents to teach and children to listen. In the course of this didactic coda, Didi's mother provided one of the most explicit statements in the Taipei materials about the links between parental care and teaching, on the one hand, and child listening, on the other. The importance of listening for the Taipei families will become even more apparent in Chapter IV where the children's participant roles are examined. For now, however, it is worth noting that Didi's mother's continuing feelings of fear and alarm incited by Didi's dangerous misbehavior may have prompted her unusually explicit explanation.

Another strategy used to end a narration was to abstract from the story an attribute of the child. As Table 4 shows, attributes occurred more frequently for the Taipei families than the Longwood families at every age, with an overall average of 0.13, compared to 0.04. In parallel with the results for the didactic coda, the distributions for the two cultural groups did not overlap.

The content of the attributes further differentiated the groups. Most of the 18 attributes assigned to the Longwood children were positive (e.g., thoughtful, good helper, brave, tough, independent, intuitive, smart, cracks people up, verbally precocious) and only 2 were negative (shy and quarrelsome). In the Taipei families, more than half of the 61 attributes were negative. Many of these negative attributes were moral (e.g., naughty, picky, precocious at blaming people, troublesome, stingy, tricky, cries a lot, wastes money, hard to please, does not listen, careless with own belongings); others involved cognitive (e.g., not smart, poor language skills) or personality attributes (e.g., stubborn, easily frightened). Most of the positive attributes were cognitive (e.g., skilled at concentrating, drawing, memorizing, putting puzzles together, spatial activities, and sports), and only a few were moral (e.g., well behaved, mature, responsible).

Most narrations in both Taipei and Longwood ended with a shift to a new topic. As shown in Table 4, the proportion of narrations ending in this manner was high across the age range (0.93–0.99) for the Longwood families, exceeding the proportions for the Taipei families at each age (0.67–0.88).

DID LONGWOOD FAMILIES CONTINUE TO PRIVILEGE A CHILD-AFFIRMING INTERPRETIVE FRAMEWORK?

The foregoing analysis not only confirmed that the Taipei families continued to privilege a didactic interpretive framework, treating young children's past transgressions as a didactic resource, but also that the Longwood families continued to enact a child-favorability bias, editing young children's past transgressions out of the narrative record. By erasing children's misdeeds, the Longwood families created recurring portraits that were favorable to their child.

But an interpretive framework that is affirming to young children could also operate in another way, namely by highlighting or inflating children's positive actions or qualities. In other words, if Longwood parents had a strong inclination to affirm children via narrative, they could realize this inclination by omitting the child's misdeeds *and* by highlighting her strengths. The Taipei families, on the other hand, might be less likely to highlight children's good deeds and accomplishments because such actions have less didactic potential or because too much focus on the positive carries the risk of diluting children's motivation for moral self-improvement. Alternatively, didactic and affirming frameworks could co-exist for the Taipei parents; they might portray their children favorably in some stories, while narrating their misdeeds in others. The following analysis was developed to explore these possibilities. Because

41

this coding scheme was new, it was applied to the complete corpus at 2,6, 3,0, 3,6, and 4,0.

Child-Affirming Codes Defined

Three new codes were employed to examine narrations of past experiences: child-positive, child-preference, and humor.

Child-Positive

This code was applied if the child was portrayed in a positive light, as interpreted from the perspective of at least one of the narrating participants. Suppose, for example, that the child was involved in preparing dinner in the kitchen. If the event was narrated in a way that implied that the child accomplished something (e.g., you were in charge of adding the sugar), behaved in a virtuous manner (e.g., you helped), or displayed some other positive quality (e.g., you knew how to stir), the story was coded "child-positive." But, if the narrator(s) characterized the child's action in neutral terms (e.g., you sat on the counter while dad made supper) or negative terms (e.g., you made a mess with the sugar), the story was not coded "child-positive." Child-positive stories were identified on the basis of the following kinds of evidence: (a) explicit positive evaluation of the child's past actions or qualities or of the child's rendition of the story. For example, Patrick's (3,6) mother related that Patrick was hospitalized a few days earlier due to his asthma. When the researcher expressed empathy, his mother commented, "He was, he was *great*...He *has no problems* with needles, doctors, and hospitals." Later in the narration Patrick said, "Yeah, and I be *brave*." In another example, Didi (3,0) was also described as brave. He and his mother co-narrated an event in which the family went swimming. Initially Didi was scared, but eventually he dared to play in the swimming pool. His mother told Didi's older sister and the researcher, "Then he became so *brave*. He walked in the water by himself, walked, walked, right?" and then said to Didi, "Oh, you were *great*, right?" (b) Implicit positive evaluation of the child's past action, as indicated by intonation, stress, gestures (e.g., hand clapping, high-five) and/or implicit verbal characterizations, including invoking admirable behaviors. Amy (3,6) initiated a narration in which she tried to recall what object was stolen from the family's vehicle when they went to the theater. Upon hearing, Amy correctly report that it was the CD player, her mother *put her thumbs up* and *spoke loudly and enthusiastically*, "The CD player! Excellent! Boy, you see those wheels turning!" Angu (3,0) accurately reported to her aunt what happened when they were at the airport a few days earlier and her aunt responded by *clapping her hands, raising her voice, smiling,* and commenting, "You got the right answer! You were right! Angu got the right answer!"

42

Child-Preference

This code was included as part of the child-affirming rubric because there is evidence that middle-class American parents and teachers encourage children to develop and express their preferences (e.g., Harwood et al., 1995; Miller et al., 2002; Tobin, 1995), reflecting the high value placed on personal choice and the expression of an inner self in North American culture (e.g., Markus & Kitayama, 1994; Savani, Markus, & Conner, 2008; Shweder et al., 2006; Taylor, 1989). This code was applied to stories in which a preference or dispreference was attributed to the child by one or more of the narrating participants, in an implicitly or explicitly accepting manner and without any expression of disapproval. Preferences could be expressed in a variety of ways, indicating that the child "likes a friend," "loves to do puzzles," "is crazy about toy cars," "wanted French fries," "insisted on going to the park," or used gestures such as head nodding. Dispreferences were similar but had a negative valence; the child "hates going to the hospital," "did not want to eat vegetables," "refused to sing," or "dislikes staying home alone." For example, Patrick's mother related that when Patrick (3,0) got his allergy shots, he was allowed to choose a reward, either dinner or a movie. Patrick responded, "Pick a movie... Yeah! Pick the real Terminator," as he stood up and punched his fists in the air. On another occasion, Patrick (2,6) and his older brother and mother recounted what they had for breakfast. Patrick said, "I had Batman cereal, too." His brother revealed, "*Patrick spit it right out!*" indicating Patrick's strong dispreference for the cereal. Similarly, Meimei's (3,0) mother commented, "*She could play [Lego blocks] by herself for a long time,* like an entire morning." When Meimei (3,6) and her mother co-narrated a trip to the zoo, Meimei said, "Mommy, bring me there. Next time, bring me there again."

For the sake of completeness, we also re-examined the child transgression stories analyzed as part of the didactic framework to determine whether child preferences were ever narrated as transgressions. In other words, children's preferences could be narrated in an accepting manner in some stories and in a disapproving manner in other stories.

Humor

This code was applied if the child was portrayed as doing or saying something funny or the entire event in which the child participated was portrayed as humorous, from the standpoint of at least one of the narrating participants. Humor stories were identified on the basis of the following kinds of evidence: (a) explicit characterization of the child's past actions, speech, or qualities as humorous or of the child's enactment of the story as humorous. For example, one of the narrating participants said, "It was so funny." "She

43

was hilarious." "We couldn't stop laughing." "He is such a clown."; (b) implicit evaluation of the child's past actions, speech, or qualities as humorous or of the enactment of the story as humorous. Specifically, humor was conveyed by laughter, intonation, stress, gestures, or sarcasm; (c) these same explicit and implicit evaluations applied when the story was about the child's participation in an amusing event. For example, Megan (3,6) initiated a story in which she related to her mother and sister a mishap that made her laugh, "And Rob (pause) his chair wasn't there and he went boom." This narration prompted laughter from all the participants and led Megan's sister to tell another story in which exactly the same thing happened to her, leading to still more laughter.

In coding the stories for the foregoing child-affirming codes, the coders did not treat the codes as mutually exclusive. In other words, any given story could receive more than one code. For example, a story might portray the child favorably and also be told humorously.

Intercoder reliabilities were determined using the same procedures described earlier. Figures ranged from 0.89 to 0.97 with a mean of 0.94 (Taipei) and 0.89 to 0.93 with a mean of 0.91 (Longwood) for child-positive, from 0.85 to 0.96, with a mean of 0.91 (Taipei) and 0.77 to 1.00 with a mean of 0.89 (Longwood) for child preference, and from 0.96 to 1.00 with a mean of 0.99 (Taipei) and 0.86 to 0.93 with a mean of 0.90 (Longwood) for humor.

Results: Child-Affirming Interpretive Framework

Child-Positive

As shown in Table 5, the Longwood families and the Taipei families produced nearly identical proportions (about .20) of stories in which the child was cast in a positive light. For the Longwood families, the proportions nearly doubled from .15 at the early ages to .28 at 4,0. For the Taipei families, the proportion of child-positive stories ranged from .12 to .23 but there was no pattern across the ages. There were also some similarities in content. Both the Longwood and Taipei families attributed cognitive competencies to their children (e.g., intelligence, good memory, large vocabulary, knowledge of body parts), recognized their attainment of developmental milestones (e.g., toilet training, transitioning from bottles to cups), and portrayed the children as virtuous (e.g., helpful, brave, honest, generous, considerate).

However, there were also notable differences in story content. The Taipei parents, but not the Longwood parents, extolled Confucian virtues such as obedience to elders, proper behavior, good habits, and "learning virtues" (Li, 2004a) such as persistence in completing tasks, patience in learning, and the

TABLE 5

FREQUENCY AND PROPORTION OF CHILD-POSITIVE, CHILD PREFERENCE, AND HUMOR AT EACH
AGE (TAIPEI/LONGWOOD)

Age	Child Positive		Child Preference		Humor	
	Frequency	Proportion	Frequency	Proportion	Frequency	Proportion
2,6	11/17	.12/.15	21/34	.23/.30	2/12	.02/.11
3,0	31/16	.23/.15	24/30	.18/.28	7/ 8	.05/.07
3,6	18/22	.17/.19	18/33	.17/.29	2/13	.02/.12
4,0	32/24	.23/.28	23/19	.17/.22	2/12	.01/.14
Total	92/79	.20/.19	86/116	.18/.28	13/45	.03/.11

ability to concentrate for extended periods of time. Some of the Taipei parents talked at length about the process by which the child had mastered a task or solved a problem. By contrast, the Longwood parents focused on inherent abilities, not on the learning process. They also affirmed their children's unique personality characteristics (e.g., being cute or funny, being a real entertainer, not being shy, having no trouble warming up).

Child-positive stories also differed qualitatively in how families narrated children's strengths. The Longwood families sometimes depicted the children in extravagantly positive terms via boasting and lavish praise. For example, Steve (3,6) and his brother were portrayed as entertaining their friend Pam by tickling her and making her laugh. In the course of this story, Steve's mother commented repeatedly on the boys' success, "And she was roaring [with laughter]. She just loved it, didn't she, boys? ... Pam was having a ball! ... She'll never forget these dudes." In another story at the same age, Steve's mother said, "They [Steve and his brother] are puzzle whizzes, I'm telling you. [To Steve] Do this. Do the Mickey Mouse one [puzzle] and show how well you do it.... It's just unbelievable how well they do these.... It just blows me away how well they can do these.... You know, in kindergarten, they have these goofy little three-piece things [puzzles]. You know these kids are putting together these, these types of [much more complex] puzzles. I just think it's great." Steve's mother depicted the boys as having extraordinary ability, and then went on to establish just how advanced their skills were. She asserted that Steve was already able to do puzzles that were much more complex than the puzzles found in kindergarten for much older children.

Another story in which a child's behavior received very positive comment involved Amy (4,0), who initiated an account of what she learned at day camp, "Once there was a fire someplace, where and someone would have to go to the fire department... That's what the policeman told me at play camp." Later in the narration, Amy's mother asked her to relate what the policeman said.

45

Example 4: Amy (4,0) receives high praise for her knowledge (excerpt from longer story)

Child:	He tell me to go to the fire department, um the police, to, if you crash, you have to call the policeman.
Mother:	If you cra, what did he say? If you crash?
Child:	If you crash you have to call the policeman, right?
Mother:	Okay, and when do you call the fire department.
Child:	When the fire is, is out.
Mother:	Oh, when there's a fire?
Child:	Yeah.
Mother:	So he would get the fire out, I see. And when would you call an ambulance?
Child:	When someone is hurt.
Mother:	Exactamundo! (Does high-five with Amy). You are the smartest, the smartest four-year-old! And there's the smartest six-year-old and the smartest two-year-old [referring to Amy's siblings].

In this story, Amy displayed her newly acquired knowledge of what to do in the event of an emergency, correctly answering most, but not all, of her mother's tutorial questions. Her mother seemed delighted with Amy's performance, crowning it with multiple expressions of enthusiastic approval. She then praised Amy's siblings for being the smartest in their age groups. This implicit social comparison was apparently offered for the sake of Amy's siblings, who, in fact, did not display any knowledge on this occasion. Having dispensed high praise to Amy in front of her siblings, Amy's mother may have wanted to forestall any inference by the siblings that they were less smart than their sister. This interpretation is consistent with Longwood mothers' expressed desire to avoid making invidious comparisons among siblings, lest their self-esteem be harmed (Miller et al., 2001; Mintz, 1999) and with other Longwood parents' use of social comparison in stories. For example, after praising Patrick (2,6) for being brave, Patrick's mother immediately praised his brother for being older and smarter.

None of the Taipei parents made comparisons that were equally favorable to both siblings. Instead, they used sibling comparisons to establish which child did better. For example, when Didi's parents co-narrated a story in which they praised him for behaving well as he made the transition to preschool, his father drew a contrast with his older sister's behavior, "[Didi behaved well] unlike his sister, [who] always cried when going to school. She started crying when she was dropped off and did not stop crying until she was picked up." But in another story, it was Didi who was compared unfavorably to his sister. Didi's father said, "Teacher, every time I hear his teacher say that Didi behaves very well. [He] cleans toys, and takes care of other little kids. But when he gets home, he does nothing [helpful]. At home, it's always his sister who is helping."

Returning again to Example 4, in addition to high praise for Amy and her siblings, there is another feature of this example that should not be overlooked. Amy answered one of her mother's questions incorrectly, saying that the firemen come "when the fire is, is out." A parent might respond in such a situation by saying, "No, that's not right. When do the firemen come?" or "No, don't they come to put the fire out?" or any number of other ways that explicitly acknowledge the error. Instead, Amy's mother responded, "Oh, when there's a fire?" to which Amy replied, "Yes," which prompted her mother to say, "So he would get the fire out, I see." She deftly corrected her daughter without ever pointing out the error, handling Amy's mistake so tactfully that it might never have happened. The effect of this kind of "erasure," especially when combined with dramatic praise, was to create a story that was uniformly favorable to Amy. Uniformly favorable stories were less common for the Taipei children, as in the example cited above in which Didi's father quoted his teacher, attesting to Didi's helpful behavior at school, but then added that Didi "does nothing [helpful]" at home.

Another difference that distinguished the Longwood stories was that family members found ways to render quite ordinary events in ways that enlarged the child protagonist's contributions. For example, when Tommy's (2,6) mother initiated a story about cooking dinner. She asked, "Who was in charge of the salt and pepper?" to which Tommy replied, "Me." She later referred to the salt and pepper as "his job." Although Tommy's contribution to the meal preparation was minimal, his mother elevated his role, glossing his contribution this way: "He was the cook tonight" and "He was the cook. He was my helper." (See Example 1 in Chapter IV for the transcript of this story.) Meimei (3,0) too participated in cooking dinner after requesting that her mother make green beans. Her mother narrated the meal preparation in detail, including finding the recipe, going to the store to buy the green beans, and preparing the beans. She described the latter step as follows, "Yes, the green beans need to be soaked afterwards. When the green beans got bigger, we put them on the stove. After putting them on the stove for cooking, we needed to add some sugar. She [Meimei] helped with adding the sugar . . . ." Although Meimei was involved throughout the meal preparation and her contribution was acknowledged, her role was not enlarged as Tommy's was.

Child-Preference

As displayed in Table 5, the Longwood families produced slightly more stories (.28) than their Taipei counterparts (.18) in which a child's preference was narrated in an accepting manner. This disparity occurred at each age. There was a slight decline with age in both sets of families. Families narrated children's preferences or dispreferences for objects (e.g., stuffed animals, puzzles, songs), events (e.g., trips to a zoo, visits to a doctor's office, Halloween party), activities (e.g., camping, biking, reading), food (e.g., sweets, vegetables), people (e.g., grandparents, neighbors, friends), and animals (e.g., dogs, birds, giraffes).

Further examination of stories involving children's preferences revealed an interesting intersection with the narrated transgression code from the didactic analysis. In one-quarter (.26) of the narrated transgression stories in Taipei, the child's preference was treated as a misdeed, compared with only a single such instance in Longwood (see Example 6 later in this chapter). This contrast is well illustrated by parental reactions to Longlong's and Tommy's clothing preferences. Longlong's mother said that Longlong (4,0) asked his grandfather to buy him a tie because he wanted to dress like his father who wore a shirt and tie to work. She then went on to relate that he even brought the tie to school, implying that he was showing off, and complained that the tie became very untidy. When the researcher asked Longlong, "Did your classmates say anything [about your tie]? " his mother answered for him, "[They] saw him like a monster."

Tommy's clothing preferences and dispreferences were narrated many times across ages and included a story about his choice of a lion costume for Halloween. However, the point of this story, as co-narrated by his mother, sister, and Tommy (3,0), was that he changed his mind about the costume when he saw himself in the mirror, pronouncing it, "dumb." On another occasion, after relating another story about Tommy's (3,6) strong feelings about what to wear, his mother lowered her voice so that Tommy could not hear and whispered to the researcher, "I am going nuts with what he's picking out. We're like, 'Oh, great, Tommy,' he's getting all these gorgeous clothes and he would like to wear green sweats about everyday...." This comment makes it clear that although Tommy's mother did not share her young son's taste in clothing, she tolerated his choices and refrained from voicing her disapproval.

Humor

As can be seen in Table 5, humor stories occurred at a relatively low rate but accounted for many more of the Longwood stories (.11), compared with the Taipei stories (.03). The disparity in favor of Longwood occurred at every age except 3,0, when the proportion of humor stories was roughly equivalent in the two sites. The proportions for the individual children for the two cultural groups did not overlap, ranging from .07 to .14 in Longwood and from .01 to .05 in Taipei. For example, Steve (3,0), his brother, and their mother co-narrated a story about the boys' zany father. Steve said, "He [Dad], he eat my pink bone," triggering laughter from all participants. Steve's mother responded, "He did! He took a bite and started chewing and I said, 'Oh, that's great. Let's show the kids how to eat dog bones.'" Then, she asked Steve, "Did he start barking?" evoking still more laughter.

ALTERNATIVE INTERPRETATIONS OF BABYISH BEHAVIOR

The results of the foregoing analyses can be summarized as follows. The Taipei families privileged a didactic interpretive framework when narrating young children's past experiences. They treated children's past misdeeds as narratable topics with pedagogical value and created stories with distinct functional and structural characteristics that matched their didactic content. They also narrated their children's strengths and accepted many of their preferences while interpreting others preferences as misdeeds. The Longwood families privileged a child-affirming interpretive framework that was distinct in its twin focus on omitting the negative and highlighting the positive. They deleted children's misdeeds and shortcomings, accentuated their strengths, accepted and almost never disapproved of their preferences, and used humor for its own sake and to downplay the negative. In other words, these analyses established that personal storytelling, as enacted by parents, siblings, and the focal children, embodied different interpretive frameworks in the two cultural cases.

In this section, we bring these alternative frameworks into sharper focus. Our analytic strategy is to compare two similar stories, one from Taipei and one from Longwood, in which the narrated event could be interpreted didactically or affirmingly. The stories in question focused on the child's failure to break a babyish habit involving a strong preference—sucking a pacifier (Meimei) or her thumb (Karen). In both instances, the child engaged in this behavior in the here-and-now (occasioning transgression), prompting a story about a similar misdeed in the past. In addition, in both stories, the child's father was invoked although he was not present during the narration. In comparing these stories, it is important to remember that Meimei's story is one of many Taipei transgression stories, whereas Karen's story is an *outlier*—a rare instance of a transgression story within the Longwood distribution, and one of only three Longwood stories in which a transgression story was preceded by an occasioning transgression. Viewed from the perspective of the child-affirming framework, however, Karen's story fits squarely within the Longwood distribution (in which preferences were almost always accepted) and Meimei's fits squarely within the Taipei distribution (in which preferences could be narrated as transgressions).

In the first example, Meimei had been engaged in drawing when she began to suck on her pacifier. Her mother rebuked her and then launched into a generic story (in bold typeface).

Example 5: Meimei (3,6) continued her bad habit of sucking on a pacifier

Child:	(Sucks on the pacifier) (Unintelligible) [Occasioning Transgression] (With the pacifier in her mouth, jumps up and down on the sofa, then runs to Mother.)
Mother:	Ay, you are acting really shameful [*xiu xiu*]. (Moves Meimei onto her lap, holds her in an upright position, and points to the camcorder) I tell you, if, if Daddy sees you do this again, ay! **You always suck on your pacifier at home, and then you tell your daddy that you do not suck on your pacifier anymore. Then you are lying, aren't you?** (While saying this, repeatedly makes a shaming gesture on Meimei's right cheek.)
Child:	(Removes pacifier from mouth. Takes away the drawing that Researcher was looking at and runs back to the center of the living room.)
Researcher:	Ay-yo, she took it [=drawing] away again.
Child:	(Takes out the pacifier, puts it on the table, and starts to add some more details to the drawing) I want (unintelligible).
Researcher:	[To Mother] **Oh, did her daddy, did her daddy ask her to quit sucking on the pacifier?**
Mother:	Yes. **[We] wanted her to quit, but she could not stop sucking on it.**
Researcher:	**Hu huh.**
Mother:	**Then we deceived her like this, we told her, "If you keep sucking on your pacifier again, then we won't bring you to America, leaving you alone here."**
Researcher:	**Did it work?**
Mother:	**[We] don't know yet.**
Child:	(Raises her head and looks at the camcorder, suggesting that she may be listening. Lowers her head and draws again.)

In this example, Meimei's mother explicitly characterized Meimei's preference as "really shameful," and forecast Meimei's father's displeasure. She then linked Meimei's here-and-now act of sucking on her pacifier to her past bad habit, via a generic story, accompanied by a shaming gesture. In this story, her mother accused her of always sucking on her pacifier and then lying to her father. Meimei's father, who was studying in the United States, regularly questioned her about her conduct during their phone conversations. Hearing her mother say this, Meimei took out the pacifier, grabbed the drawing from the researcher, ran away from her mother and the researcher, and engaged in more drawing. In response to a question from the researcher, Meimei's mother explained that she and her husband wanted the child to give up the pacifier. Then she quoted the threat that they made to persuade Meimei to stop her bad habit: "If you keep sucking on your pacifier, then we won't bring you to America, leaving you alone here." Meimei raised her head and gazed at the adults, suggesting that she might have been listening to their conversation. Then she looked down and resumed drawing. Seen as a whole, the most striking feature of this episode is the density and variety of ways in which Meimei's mother conveyed the seriousness of Meimei's bad habit: verbal and nonverbal shaming, invoking the displeasure of Meimei's absent father, linking Meimei's use of the pacifier to the more serious transgression of lying, and threatening to leave her behind when the family moved to America.

Karen's Thumb Sucking

Karen's family adopted a dramatically different attitude toward her bad habit of thumb sucking. Before turning to the example, it is important to note that this family's lighthearted response to Karen's thumb sucking was expressed in a longstanding family routine. When Karen was 2,6, her mother asked her, "What does Daddy say?" to which Karen replied, "Get that thumb out of that mouth!" Mother and child then proceeded to relate that Karen laughed when her father told her to get her thumb out of her mouth, her father then put *his* thumb in *his* mouth, and Karen scolded him, "Get that thumb out of your mouth!"

In the later example, which is the focus of our comparison with Meimei's story, the lead-up to the story unfolded as follows: Karen and the researcher were in the living room while Karen's mother was busy preparing food in the kitchen, within earshot of the living room conversation. Karen was lying on the sofa, sucking her thumb. When she responded unintelligibly to a question from the researcher, her mother intervened from the kitchen, "Get that thumb out of your mouth and tell us where did you go?" Karen took out her thumb, said, "went to church," and stuck it back in. The following exchange occurred 45 seconds later.

Example 6: Karen (3,0) continued her "bad" habit of sucking her thumb. Story is in boldface.

Child: (Unintelligible) (Talks with her thumb in her mouth) [Occasioning Transgression]

51

Researcher:	What? I cannot hear that with your thumb in your mouth.
Child:	(Thumb still in the mouth) "No thumb in your mouth."
Researcher:	(Laughs).
Mother:	(Approaches Karen from the kitchen and then shifts her into a sitting position) Get that thumb out of your mouth and get up so that J [= Researcher] can see you.
Researcher:	(Laughs) [To Mother] **I got to hear her dad say that to her the other day.**
Child:	[To Researcher] Can you see me?
Researcher:	Uh huh.
Child:	See.
Researcher:	**What did your dad say to you when I was here?**
Mother:	(Unintelligible).
Researcher:	**When you were going like this.** (Imitates Karen's thumb sucking)
Child:	**What?**
Researcher:	**What did your dad say?**
Mother:	**What does Dad say? Get that (pause)**
Child:	**Thumb out** (pause)
Mother:	**Thumb out of your mouth.**
Child:	**Get that thumb out of your mouth!**
Researcher:	**He tried but did she take it out?**
Mother:	**Uh.**
Researcher:	**Hmm mm.**
Mother:	**Did she listen? No. (Laughs)**
Child:	**No!** (Laughs)
Researcher:	(Laughs)
Child:	(Takes her thumb out of her mouth and looks at Researcher and smiles).

When Karen's thumb interfered again with intelligible speech, the researcher, following the mother's example, intervened, laughing. Karen's mother repeated her earlier reprimand, "Get that thumb out of your mouth . . . " The researcher noted that she heard Karen's father say the same thing to Karen a few days earlier, referencing another instance of the family routine, and then joined in the routine by trying to get Karen to repeat the reprimand. Karen's mother stepped in and prompted the well-worn phrase ("Get that thumb out of your mouth"), which culminated in Karen gleefully quoting her father, "Get that thumb out of your mouth!" When the researcher asked whether Karen complied, her mother matter-of-factly admitted that she did not and Karen added a gleeful, "No!" In other words, Example 6 continued a double routine: Karen's parents playfully scolded her for thumb sucking *and* told stories about these amusing events. In contrast to the Meimei example, Karen's preference for thumb sucking had become something of a family joke, a joke that had been going on for at least 6 months.

This playful routine was sustained by the coordinated efforts of the various participants—Karen's mother, Karen herself, and even the researcher—just as Meimei's mother, Meimei herself, and the researcher contributed to Meimei's story. However, their participation yielded qualitatively different interpretations of the child's babyish behavior. The didactic slant took precedence for Meimei's mother, who interpreted Meimei's behavior as a transgression, pure, and simple; the fact that Meimei had a strong attachment to the pacifier was not a mitigating factor. In Karen's case, all of the narrating participants acknowledged that her thumb sucking was unacceptable ("Get that thumb out of that mouth!"), but this "rule" was keyed humorously on each iteration, cancelling its literal meaning and thereby affirming Karen's preference. Adding weight to this reading is the difference in how the fathers were represented: as a judging witness in Meimei's case and a co-participant in subversive play in Karen's. Although neither little girl seemed inclined to give up her babyish habit, noncompliance put Meimei, but not Karen, at odds with parental authority.

DISCUSSION

The findings of this chapter form a complex pattern of similarities and differences in the practice of personal storytelling in Taipei and Longwood, a pattern that parallels and extends our earlier findings when the children were 2,6 (Miller et al., 1996, 1997).

Personal Storytelling Continued

Every family in the two sites routinely narrated children's past experiences at 3,0, 3,6, and 4,0, just as they had at 2,6. Moreover, the overall patterns in terms of frequency and length were remarkably similar. Stories about children's past experiences occurred at roughly four to five times per hour and averaged 15 to 16 utterances per narration. Age patterns within each group showed some minor differences. For the Taipei families, frequency and story length were lowest at the youngest age. However, for Longwood, the frequency of stories declined at the oldest age; at 4,0 they produced a relatively small number of relatively long stories. We will address this finding in more detail in Chapter IV. In short, the practice of telling stories about young children's past experiences remained a robust part of everyday life throughout the preschool years, establishing personal storytelling as a socializing pathway in both Taipei and Longwood.

In counterpoint to this similarity, we found that the Taipei and Longwood families continued to enact different frameworks or lenses for interpreting children's past experience. The privileging of the didactic framework in the Taipei stories occurred at all levels of analysis. Turning first to content, the Taipei families continued to narrate children's past transgressions much more frequently than their Longwood counterparts—at least five times more frequently at every age. However, this dramatic quantitative difference conveys only part of the picture; the stories also differed qualitatively. This was most apparent in microlevel analysis of how similar childish behaviors were narrated: Meimei's mother called her daughter's continued use of her pacifier "shameful" and linked it to a second serious transgression (lying to her father), whereas Karen's mother made light of her daughter's continued thumb sucking, and admitted, without apparent concern, that Karen defied her parents' playful scolding. The Taipei families used shaming, power assertion, and love withdrawal to communicate their strong disapproval of children's misdeeds and to insist that the child cease misbehaving. By contrast, on the rare occasions that the Longwood parents narrated their children's past transgressions, they *downplayed* the seriousness of the past misdeed—framing the misdeed humorously, putting a positive spin on it, or expressing their love for the child despite the misdeed—just as they had when the children were 2,6.

These differences in what was said, how it was said, and what was omitted, confirm, and extend our earlier findings, suggesting that personal storytelling with young children indexed different cultural meanings in Taipei and Longwood. As presented in Chapter II, the Taipei parents grew up in an era in which the government promoted Confucian principles as a way to create a Chinese version of modernity, embracing the Confucian idea of shame as a virtue (Fung, 1999). Thus, it is not surprising that parents held their young children to high standards in the narrative medium. Their frequent narration of young children's misdeeds, along with their use of strategies that emphasized the serious consequences of wrongdoing, are consistent with the importance accorded to children's moral education in the Confucian tradition (Fung, Leiber, & Leung, 2003; Li, 2002, 2003a, 2003b, 2004a; Lieber, Fung, & Leung, 2006) and, specifically, with the idea that such education should begin early (Fung, 1994, 1999). According to Wu (1996), Confucian tradition holds that moral learning is required to become human and should "begin early enough in the family to lay the foundation for the child to become a future adult of proper manners and moral tenets" (p. 144). This tradition also places a high value on didactic written narrative in conveying moral tenets to children (Fung et al., 2004; Miller et al., 1997; Wu, 1996).

The results of the functional analysis lend further support to these interpretations. Not only did the Taipei families tell many more stories in which they cast the child protagonist as a transgressor, communicating the seriousness of his or her misbehavior, but they were also much more likely to treat the child's misdeeds in the here-and-now as occasions to remind the child of a previous misdeed. This almost never happened in Longwood. The pattern enacted by the Taipei parents instantiated *jihui jiaoyu* (opportunity education), a teaching strategy that these and other parents endorsed in interviews about childrearing (Fung, 1999). Opportunity education involves two interlinked ideas: that it is more effective to situate a moral lesson in the child's concrete experience than to preach in the abstract and that parents should take every opportunity to do so. The results of this chapter suggest that the Taipei parents used stories in exactly this way and that they did so throughout the age range.

Opportunity education also draws our attention to the socializing power of recurring juxtapositions of different types of discursive practice (see Fung & Chen, 2001). Opportunity education entailed the systematic real-time linking of one morally inflected discursive practice (rebuking the child for a here-and-now misdeed) with another (narrating the same child's past misdeed). Each instance of opportunity education involved the higher order packaging and repackaging of pointed moral messages about the child's own actions. When parents seized upon a child's current misdeed and linked it to a misdeed that she had committed at an earlier time, they rehearsed, reinforced, and enriched particular moral messages while also adapting those messages to the current context. These redundant yet variable discursive strategies may cultivate in the child an alertness to the moral domain and an awareness of herself as a moral actor. We will return to these points in Chapter V.

The analysis of story endings added one more piece of evidence to the divergent messages conveyed in the two sets of stories. Although the majority of stories ended with interruptions or shifts of topics, the Taipei families were more likely than their Longwood counterparts to end stories with a moral fillip: they ascribed an enduring attribute, especially a negative moral quality, to the child, and they created didactic codas in which they elaborated the implications of the child's misdeed for the present or the future. Some didactic codas were long, amounting to an extra structural component, which the Longwood stories lacked, and some offered explicit commentary on parents' motivations. By explaining to the child what he did wrong, how the misdeed could harm himself or others, and why it is important for young children to listen to their parents, they cast themselves as moral guardians to the child, as moral novice.

Longwood Families Continued to Privilege a Child-Affirming Interpretive Framework

As the foregoing section implies, the application of the didactic codes to the Longwood stories supplied the first piece of evidence pointing to the salience of a different interpretive framework in Longwood. In essence, these codes, which captured important patterns in the Taipei stories, did not "fit" the Longwood stories at 2,6 (Miller et al., 1996, 1997) and this lack of fit continued at 3,0, 3,6, and 4,0. To put this another way, the fact that young children's misdeeds were systematically, prolifically, and elaborately narrated in one cultural case allowed us to see their systematic omission in the other. And, indeed, this difference has turned out to be the most pronounced of all the differences reported in this chapter. Thus, one critically important element in the Longwood families' child-affirming interpretive framework was the child-favorability bias created by *not* narrating children's transgressions. Moreover, the results of the new analyses of child-affirmation revealed a more general child-favorability bias by which children's errors, inaccuracies, and shortcomings were also omitted along with their misdeeds.

In addition to editing children's misdeeds out of the narrative record, the Longwood families also differed from their Taipei counterparts in accentuating the positive. This qualitative difference was achieved in a number of ways, ranging from the dramatically explicit to the exceedingly subtle. Although the Taipei families were just as likely as the Longwood families to credit children with accomplishments, positive qualities, and good deeds, the Longwood families sometimes resorted to boasting and extravagant praise. But they also deftly crafted story lines and commentaries that were discreetly favorable to the child. They seemed to be as alert and creative in their efforts to affirm their children as the Taipei parents were to teach theirs. This is also apparent in their handling of sibling comparisons. In keeping with their expressed desire to avoid invidious comparisons (Miller et al., 2001), mothers crafted comparisons that were affirming to all. If one sibling received high praise, mothers offered equivalent praise to the other or credited her with a different but equivalent strength.

The new child-affirming codes developed for this chapter also fleshed out other elements in the interpretive framework favored by the Longwood families. The Longwood families affirmed the children's preferences at a somewhat higher rate than the Taipei families, and they almost never disapproved of children's preferences. By contrast, the Taipei parents were not reluctant to disapprove of children's preferences; one quarter of the narrated transgressions were child preferences. The Longwood parents tolerated babyish preferences and preferences with which they strongly disagreed. From the perspective of the Taipei parents, this tolerant attitude might have felt like an evasion of parental responsibility and lowering of moral standards. In short, the message about preferences conveyed through Longwood narrative practices was one of broad acceptance of children's likes and dislikes, however quirky.

The final difference that emerged from the analysis of child-affirmation was that the Longwood families were more likely than the Taipei families to express humor when narrating young children's past experiences. In some cases, the point of the story was simply to savor a funny moment. The most hilarious stories, as when Steve's father ate a dog bone, caused all participants to dissolve in laughter. Humor was also used to forestall an unfavorable interpretation or inject a light note into a story that otherwise would have been unflattering to the child. The stories about Karen's thumb sucking illustrate this especially well. Karen's parents might have wished that she would stop sucking her thumb, but they handled the matter by establishing family routines, both narrative and nonnarrative, in which everyone could laugh about her behavior and her father's prohibition of it. This story neatly weaves together many of the elements of the child-affirming interpretive framework: Karen's family "canceled" her misdeed by making it the topic of a recurring joke, transformed her father's prohibition into a source of amusement, and conveyed their acceptance of her desire to retain a babyish source of comfort.

Taken together, these findings show that the Longwood families operated with a child-affirming interpretive framework that filtered out young children's transgressions and shortcomings, inflated or discreetly highlighted their strengths, accepted children's preferences, and encouraged humor. The steady enactment of this interpretive framework across the entire age range offers further support for a convergence between narrative practices and the Longwood mothers' avowed goal of cultivating their children's self-esteem, in contrast to the way they had been raised (Miller et al., 2001; Mintz, 1999) (see Chapter II). These findings also add important new evidence to the emerging consensus that parents from a variety of European-American communities place a premium on fostering children's self-esteem, compared with their counterparts in Taiwan, China, Greece, Puerto Rico, and other cultures (e.g., Harwood et al., 1995; Miller, et al., 2002; Stevenson & Stigler, 1992; Tamis-LeMonda et al., 2002).

At the same time, our findings add an important warning against depicting such comparisons in either/or terms. Although the didactic interpretive framework took precedence for the Taipei families, their assiduous use of children's misdeeds as teaching opportunities did not prevent them from narrating their children's cognitive and moral strengths; praising them for their persistence, concentration, and patience in learning; and recognizing their preferences and dispreferences. Thus, the Taipei children could find in personal storytelling many messages about where they fell short and how they could improve as well as messages about what they did well. For the

Longwood children, personal storytelling served mainly as a source of favorable messages. Future work will have to examine other discursive practices to determine when Longwood children receive negative feedback and how they respond.

It is also important to keep in mind that the interpretive frameworks that we have focused on in this chapter, however culturally salient, do not exhaust the full range and variety of interpretive frameworks that could be examined. Every culture has multiple interpretive frameworks, reflecting the complex needs of social life and the contradictions in value systems (Briggs, 1998; Lutz & White, 1986), and creating ambiguity in any cultural practice, including narrative (Hanks, 1996; Miller & Goodnow, 1995).

In sum, this chapter established that the Taipei and Longwood youngsters inhabited home environments in which personal storytelling was part and parcel of everyday life. The most significant finding of this chapter is that the pattern of similarities and differences in personal storytelling was remarkably stable during the preschool years, creating distinct developmental pathways for the Taipei and Longwood children. The steady recurrence of culturally saturated stories, from 2,6 to 4,0, afforded the children an enormous number of opportunities to hear which of their own past experiences were narratable and how these experiences were interpreted by significant others. In the next chapter, we ask how the children participated in these practices and how their participation changed over time.

IV. PARTICIPANT ROLES

Shumin Lin, Peggy J. Miller, Heidi Fung, and Eva Chian-Hui Chen

In this chapter, we analyze how the children participated in personal storytelling. As explained in Chapter I, by taking a different analytic perspective on the entire corpus, this analysis was intended to enrich our understanding of how personal storytelling was practiced with young children. Moreover, the issue of children's participant roles is particularly interesting, given emerging evidence that cultural models of Taiwanese communicative style privilege listening over speaking while the converse applies in the United States. We asked two questions: What kinds of participant roles were available to the Taipei and Longwood children? And how did their participation change during the preschool years? Again, we organize the chapter by question. For each question, we first define and illustrate the codes and then present the results. The chapter concludes with a brief discussion of the results; we also take up the question of how the results of this chapter converge with the results of Chapter III.

WHAT KINDS OF PARTICIPANT ROLES WERE AVAILABLE TO THE CHILDREN?

We examined the transcribed stories to determine the ways in which children participated in stories of their past experiences. We found two types: (a) the child participated as a *co-narrator*, and (b) the child participated as a *bystander*. In the co-narrator role, the child contributed at least two substantive, on-topic utterances, and other speakers primarily referred to the child protagonist in the second person. In the bystander role, the child was present within earshot of a narration that a family member addressed to another person(s), primarily referring to the child in the third person. In this configuration, the focal child made little (a maximum of one substantive utterance) or no verbal contribution to the story.

In the following example, Tommy participated as a co-narrator, as he and his mother together related an event about cooking dinner together. Tommy contributed four substantive, on-topic utterances (in bold typeface) and his mother primarily referred to him in the second person (you).

Example 1: Tommy (2,6) as a co-narrator

Mother:	Who was in charge of the salt and pepper?
Child:	**Me.**
Mother:	Who, what did you do?
Child:	(Makes shaking motion)
Mother:	He was the cook tonight.
Sibling:	Could I (unintelligible) the (unintelligible)?
Mother:	Yeah, in a minute. Tommy's telling us. How did we make the potatoes?
Child:	**Um, good.**
Mother:	Oh, we made 'em good. How did we make them?
Child:	**Um, mash them.**
Mother:	Kind of cut them up and then what was your job?
Child:	**Salt and pepper.**
Mother:	You were the salt and pepper. You had to shake the salt and pepper all over the potatoes.
Researcher:	That's a very important job.
Mother:	He was the cook. He was my helper.

If Tommy's mother had narrated the story to another person in the third person ("Last night Tommy helped me cook. We made mashed potatoes and then he was in charge of the salt and pepper . . . ") while Tommy was playing silently with his toy cars a few feet away, Tommy's role would have been coded as bystander.

The next example illustrates the bystander role. As Longlong's (2,6) mother told the researcher about how Longlong broke the tapes that she bought, Longlong was within earshot of the narration, playing with his toy. He did not contribute any utterances, and his mother referred to him in the third person (he/him).

Example 2: Longlong (2,6) as a bystander

Mother:	The audio, audiotapes about children's songs that I bought have been broken by him. Each tape is worth over one hundred dollars!
Researcher:	(Laughs)
Mother:	He just pulled the tape out, and it's broken.
Researcher:	Oh, he pulled the tape out, out, out.
Mother:	Yes. He pulled all the tapes out. He broke at least four of them.
Researcher:	(Laughs)

The intercoder reliability procedures described in Chapter III were followed for the coding of co-narrator and bystander roles (and for all codes presented in this chapter). In each site at each age, at least one fourth of all stories were coded by two independent coders, and proportions of agreement were computed. These ranged from 0.91 to 1.00 with a mean of 0.94 (Taipei) and from 0.95 to 0.96 with a mean of 0.96 (Longwood).

The results of the analysis of co-narrator and bystander roles are displayed in Table 6. In both communities, children were afforded both participant roles across the entire age range. However, the proportions differed quite dramatically. In Taipei, the bystander role predominated over the co-narrator role at every age, with a range of 0.55 to 0.62 for the bystander role and 0.38 to 0.45 for the co-narrator role. In Longwood, the two roles were balanced at 2,6 and 3,0, but the co-narrator role predominated over the bystander role at 3,6 (0.58 vs. 0.42) and 4,0 (0.73 vs. 0.27). In other words, in the Taipei families, the bystander role continued to be an important participation route throughout the entire age range, coexisting with the co-narrator route. By contrast, the bystander role seemed to ebb over time for the Longwood children, creating a pattern of increasing ascendancy of the co-narrator role.

When these patterns are viewed in conjunction with the patterns for absolute frequencies, a few additional details emerge (see Table 6). Overall, summing across the four ages, Taipei produced many more stories in which the children were cast as bystanders (Taipei: 278 vs. Longwood: 180) and Longwood produced more stories in which the children were cast as co-narrators (Longwood: 240 vs. Taipei: 192). In addition, although the bystander role predominated across the age range for the Taipei children, there was an increase in the absolute frequencies of both the bystander role and the co-narrator role from 2,6 to 4,0. The means and medians show parallel patterns (see Table 6). In the Longwood case, there was little change in the absolute frequencies of the co-narrator role but a decrease in those of the bystander role from 2,6 to 4,0. Again, the means and medians showed parallel patterns. Moreover, when the 24 individual data points were examined (six children at four age points for each cultural group), the co-narrator role predominated in 15 data points for Longwood and the bystander role predominated in 16 data points for Taipei.

In sum, during the entire period from 2,6 to 4,0, all of the children participated routinely in personal storytelling as both co-narrators and bystanders. However, this similarity coexisted with a robust pattern of difference such that the Taipei children experienced more stories from the vantage point of the bystander role, whereas the Longwood children experienced more stories from the vantage point of the co-narrator role.

TABLE 6
Frequencies, Proportions, Means, and Medians of Participant Roles by Age and Site (Taipei/Longwood)

Age	Co-Narrator				Bystander				Total
	Frequency	Proportion	Mean	Median	Frequency	Proportion	Mean	Median	
2,6	35/57	.38/.51	5.8/9.5	3.0/7.0	57/55	.62/.49	9.2/9.2	9.5/6.5	92/112
3,0	51/55	.39/.50	8.5/9.2	6.0/7.5	81/54	.61/.50	13.5/9.0	13.5/8.0	132/109
3,6	48/65	.40/.58	7.2/10.8	7.0/10.0	64/48	.60/.42	10.7/8.0	8.5/7.5	107/113
4,0	63/63	.45/.73	10.5/10.5	9.5/10.0	76/23	.55/.27	12.7/3.8	12.5/3.5	139/86
Total	192/240	.41/.57	–	–	278/180	.59/.43	–	–	470/420

HOW DID THE CHILDREN'S PARTICIPATION CHANGE OVER TIME?

Having established that two participant roles were available to the children, we next asked how their participation changed within the context of each of these roles. Did the children become more active within the co-narrator and bystander roles? And did each group have an advantage with respect to the participant role that afforded them more experience, that is, the co-narrator role for the Longwood children and the bystander role for the Taipei children?

Being Active in the Co-Narrator Role: Codes Defined

We defined *activeness* within the co-narrator role according to the following four dimensions that capture the ways in which children exercised agency or exerted control over the narration.

Initiating

The focal child introduced a story on a new topic. For example, Amy (2,6) launched a story on a new topic by saying "A tree fell down." Then she and her mother and brother co-narrated a story of how a tree outside their house was struck by a car and Amy tried to "fix" the tree. In another example, after discussing the differences between a supermarket and a traditional market with his brother and mother, Yoyo (4,0) initiated a story on a related but new topic, "I still remember I fell down one day." Then all three participants co-narrated how Yoyo stood in the cart when shopping with his mother and fell off when the cart tilted.

Authoring

The child was chiefly responsible for narrating the story. Specifically, he or she contributed more turns that included new information than his or her co-narrator contributed. If the story included two or more co-narrators (e.g., mother and sibling) in addition to the focal child, the focal child had to contribute more turns of new information than both co-narrators combined. Thus, this was a stringent definition of authoring. A turn of new information was defined as any turn in which the child produced information not previously introduced by a co-narrator. If the child provided multiple turns in which he repeated new information, he was credited with a single turn. When the child responded to a co-narrator's questions, two conditions were considered: (a) When the questions were "yes/no" questions, the co-narrator's turn was counted as providing new information while the child's turn was not;

(b) when the questions were "wh-" questions, both the co-narrator's and the child's turns were counted as providing new information. Below is an example of how turns of new information were counted. The bold parts are the focal child's turns of new information; the italic parts are the co-narrator's.

Example 3: Yoyo (4,0) authored a story

Child:	**Don't be like me. One day I went to a place to eat ice popsicles and the water dropped, and made me wet.**
Researcher:	Really? *Where?*
Child:	**In a small park.**
Researcher:	In a small park. Oh. And *it dropped on the ground?* And it dropped on you.
Child:	**And I ate bubble gums too.**
Researcher:	Oh. And bubble gums.
Child:	**And I dropped it on my hand and then I ate it.**
Researcher:	And you dropped it on your hand and then you ate it.

The child was credited with authoring the story because he contributed four turns containing new information, compared with the researcher, who contributed two turns. In Example 4 below Megan authored a story with her mother.

Example 4: Megan (4,0) authored a story

Child:	**Once Maggie and I landed on free when they were having a sleepover and it was morning time and we played this game.**
Mother:	Yeah.
Child:	**And um Maggie landed on free and so Maggie landed on free and she spinned again and then Johnny went and then it landed on free then Johnny (unintelligible) and then put it in.**
Mother:	*Put it in where?*
Child:	He put (interrupted).
Mother:	*In somebody else's barrel?*
Child:	**No! Johnny won the first time when we had the sleepover. And that's all.**
Mother:	Oh okay.

In this example, Megan was credited with contributing three turns of new information, whereas her mother contributed only two turns.

Questioning

The focal child made one or more queries during the co-narration. All but a few took the form of questions (wh-questions, yes/no questions, tag questions). Questions were used to express curiosity or to seek information, clarification, or verification about what happened in the past event or to seek clarification about the co-narrator's rendition. After Longlong (3,0) and his mother co-narrated their activities in a department store, Longlong asked a question seeking more information about the past event, "Mom, where else did we go?" In another example, Megan (3,0) and her sister co-narrated their experience about buying something. Megan was not sure where they made the purchase, so she asked for verification, "We got (unintelligible) from (unintelligible) mart, right, Jill?"

Resisting

The focal child refused to participate in the narration, challenged a co-narrator's accuracy or interpretation, or objected to continuing the story. For instance, when co-narrating a story about his birthday party, Steve (4,0) challenged the veracity of his mother's version of who attended the party and then went on to support his claim with supporting information.

Example 5: Steve (4,0) challenged his mother's version (excerpt of longer story)

Mother:	And who else?
Child:	And Dana.
Mother:	No, Dana wasn't there.
Child:	**Yeah.**
Mother:	No, she was not.
Child:	**Mom when (unintelligible) you were out (unintelligible), you were at work with daddy and we decided to build (unintelligible) we started. Tommy stayed here and Dana came to (pause) the party and Brooky and Dana.**

In another example, Didi (3,0) refused to continue narrating a fight that he had with his classmate. He said to his mother, "I don't want to talk any more . . . . I don't want to tell sister about it." Apparently he saw his older sister enter the living room and begin to walk toward him and his co-narrators. His mother then offered the researcher her interpretation of Didi's refusal to continue the story, "He didn't want to tell his sister about it. Every time she contradicts him."

In addition to verbal resistance, the children sometimes resisted non-verbally (e.g., Jingjing (4,0) refused to participate in a narration by putting her hand in front of the video recorder and ignoring her mother's repeated requests for her to relate how she got her towel moldy). Rarely, they used rhetorical questions to challenge a co-narrator (e.g., Angu [4,0] said, "Why didn't you reason with me nicely?!") (see Example 7 in Chapter V).

The transcript of each story in which the child participated as a co-narrator was examined to determine whether each of the four codes of child activeness applied. Then, proportions were calculated for each age within each group as well as overall proportions for each group. In addition, as a general measure of activeness, we tallied the number of stories in which the children exhibited at least one type of activeness; again we calculated proportions for each age within each group as well as overall proportions for each group.

Intercoder reliability estimates were calculated following the procedures described in Chapter III. These were 1.00 at every age (Taipei) and ranged from 0.94 to 1.00 with a mean of 0.99 (Longwood) for initiating; from 0.93 to 1.00 with a mean of 0.98 (Taipei) and from 0.93 to 1.00 with a mean of 0.97 (Longwood) for authoring; from 0.82 to 1.00 with a mean of 0.93 (Taipei) and 0.88 to 1.00 with a mean of 0.94 (Longwood) for questioning, and from 0.81 to 1.00 with a mean of 0.91 (Taipei) and from 0.86 to 1.00 with a mean of 0.92 (Longwood) for resisting.

As can be seen in Table 7, results indicated that the Taipei and Longwood children exhibited at least one type of activeness in about 0.40 of all co-narrations. However, the pattern differed across ages, with the rates increasing steadily for the Taipei children at 2,6, 3,0, 3,6 and 4,0 but remaining stable for the Longwood children. Turning to the individual categories of activeness, the Taipei and Longwood families were generally similar in both the overall rates of the categories and in their rank ordering: initiation of stories was the most frequent category, questioning was the least frequent, with authoring and resisting in between. Yet there were also differences between the two groups. Below we examine these patterns more closely for each type of activeness (see Table 7).

Results: Being Active in the Co-Narrator Role

Initiating

Although the Taipei children had relatively less experience of the co-narrator role, they initiated stories at a similar overall rate (0.22) as the Longwood children (0.23). However, the two groups showed very different patterns across the age groups. The Taipei children increased in their initiation of stories, with an average rate of 0.33 at 4,0. By contrast, the Longwood children decreased in their initiation of stories from 2,6 to 4,0, with the rates dropping to 0.10 at 4,0. It should be noted that although the rate of story initiation by the Longwood children decreased sharply at 4,0, the average length of stories produced in the Longwood families increased (see Chapter III).

TABLE 7

FREQUENCIES AND PROPORTIONS OF TYPES OF CHILDREN'S ACTIVE PARTICIPATION IN THE CO-NARRATOR ROLE IN TAIPEI AND LONGWOOD (TAIPEI/LONGWOOD)

Age	Baseline	Coding Scheme				
		Initiating	Authoring	Questioning	Resisting	All Types
2,6	35/57	6 (.17)/19 (.33)	2 (.06)/2 (.04)	2 (.06)/3 (.05)	4 (.11)/7 (.12)	.31/.46
3,0	51/55	8 (.16)/17 (.31)	3 (.06)/8 (.15)	4 (.08)/5 (.09)	11 (.22)/7 (.13)	.37/.44
3,6	43/65	8 (.19)/13 (.20)	3 (.07)/12 (.18)	4 (.09)/5 (.08)	7 (.16)/7 (.11)	.44/.43
4,0	63/63	21 (.33)/6 (.10)	12 (.19)/10 (.16)	5 (.08)/9 (.14)	17 (.27)/9 (.14)	.54/.38
Total	192/240	43 (.22)/55 (.23)	20 (.10)/32 (.13)	15 (.08)/22 (.09)	39 (.20)/30 (.13)	.42/.43

Note.—"All Types" provides the proportion of stories in which the children produced at least one type of activeness within the story; that is, they were credited with at least one of the types of active participation. The base numbers do not sum to 100 because the child may have engaged in multiple types of activeness (e.g., initiating and questioning) in a given story.

Furthermore, at 2,6 and 3,0, the Longwood children did twice as much initiating as the Taipei children, both proportionately and in absolute terms. The rates began to even out at 3,6 and reversed at 4,0, with the Taipei children initiating three times as many stories as their Longwood counterparts. In other words, the Longwood children showed an advantage early on, but the Taipei children surpassed them at 4,0.

Authoring

Although the Taipei children had relatively less experience of the co-narrator role, they authored stories at a similar overall rate (0.10) as the Longwood children did (0.13). In addition, both groups of children authored very few stories at 2,6 but by 4,0, the rate had increased by more than threefold. However, the rate for the Taipei children remained low at 2,6, 3,0, and 3,6 and only increased at 4,0. By contrast, the increase occurred at 3,0 for the Longwood children and remained stable through 4,0.

Questioning

The overall rates of questioning were low in both cultural groups: 0.08 for Taipei and 0.09 for Longwood. The Taipei children's rates of questioning were stable across the four ages, whereas the Longwood children showed an increase. At 4,0, the Longwood children produced questions in 0.14 of their co-narrations, compared with 0.08 for Taipei.

Resisting

The overall rates at which the focal child engaged in resistance during the co-narrations were slightly higher for the Taipei children (0.20) than for the Longwood children (0.13). The Taipei children's rates of resistance fluctuated across the four ages, whereas the rates were stable over time for the Longwood children.

In sum, both the Taipei and Longwood children participated actively in the co-narrator role throughout the period from 2,6 to 4,0, engaging in some form of active participation in about 0.40 of all co-narrations. Overall, they were most active as initiators of stories and least active as questioners. In addition, both groups of children authored very few stories at 2,6, but by 4,0, their rates of authorship had increased three- or fourfold. However, there were differences between the groups in the age-related patterns with respect to the other categories of activeness: the Taipei children showed an increase in initiation, stability in questioning, and an uneven but relatively high pattern of resistance, whereas the Longwood children showed a decline in initiation, an increase in questioning, and stability in resistance.

Although the co-narrator role was privileged over the bystander role in the Longwood families, affording the Longwood children more experience of the co-narrator role, they did not show a marked advantage over their Taipei counterparts. Except for questioning, the Taipei children showed at least as much activeness by 4,0 as the Longwood children. However, the Longwood children did attain relatively high rates of initiating and authoring at earlier ages.

Being Active in the Bystander Role

In the role of bystander, the child was present within earshot while another person narrated a past experience from the child's life. Such "overheard" stories about themselves appear to be especially interesting to children (e.g., Miller, 1994; Miller et al., 1990). The primary way in which children can be active within the bystander role is by listening (Fung et al., 2004).

It is not easy to determine whether a child is listening. Sometimes young children give no discernible evidence of listening—indeed, they may appear to be engrossed in some other activity—only to reveal later that they caught the gist, or even the details, of an overheard conversation (Miller et al., 1990). The problem is amplified by the constraints of recording young, active children as they interacted with others in relatively small spaces. We did not always capture the child's facial expression, and the resolution was not always adequate to capture shifts in gaze. Thus, for the purposes of this analysis, we credited the child with listening if he or she made at least one relevant verbal or nonverbal response to the story, exclusive of shifts in gaze. If no such responses occurred, the child was not credited with listening.

Relevant verbal responses included an answer to a question posed by the narrator, a verbal contribution to the story, a repetition of the narrator's utterance, or a question about the story. If the child objected verbally to a story or tried to divert the narrator from a topic she did not want to hear, this was also considered a sign of listening. (Note that such utterances were not considered to be "substantive" utterances for the purpose of the coding of co-narrator and bystander roles.) Nonverbal signs of listening included nods or head shakes to a "yes" or "no" question from the narrator, retrieving an object that was mentioned in the story, responding with an emotion appropriate to the content of the story (e.g., screaming or covering the narrator's mouth in response to a story that caused the child anger or embarrassment). For example, in one story, Meimei (3,6) hid behind the refrigerator when her mother narrated an unflattering story in which she described Meimei's behavior as manipulative and characterized her as "very bad."

In the following example, Didi indicated several times (in bold typeface) that he was listening to the story narrated by his father and his sister.

Example 6: Didi (3,0) listened when his father and sister narrated his experience

Father: Didi, was there anyone borrowing your pants?

Sister: Yes, there was.

Child: **(Nods and stands up)**

Father: Did you tell auntie [the researcher] about it yet?

Child: **(Runs to a corner of the dining area) I don't want to [tell the story]. (Hides behind a wall)**

Researcher: (Laughs) Someone borrowed his pants? Did that boy wet his?

Father: Yes, that boy wet his own pants, you know. He wet his pants, and he had no other pants to change.

Researcher: (Laughs) Oh.

Father: We prepared two pairs of pants for him [Didi]. The teacher borrowed one pair from him. And then the teacher told him, "You tell your father and mother about this when you get home."

Researcher: Yes.

Father: And then when I went to pick him up, he told me, "A boy wet his pants, loaned a pair of pants to him." (Speaks loudly when quoting)

Researcher: (Laughs)

Sister: A boy wet his pants (speaks loudly). Don't lend yours to him.

Father: Yes.

Sister: This is (pause).

Father: (Ignores sister) He loaned his pants to him.

Sister: Yeah.

Father: But I was not clear. I asked him, "Did you loan [the pants to] him or did the teacher loan [them to] him?" I (pause).

Child: **(Steps out from his hiding place) It's the teacher, it's the teacher who loaned the pants.** (Narration continues)

The first indication that Didi was listening occurred early in the narration when he nodded in response to a question from his father. Two turns later, Didi explicitly objected to the story ("I don't want to [tell the story].") and hid behind a wall, thereby removing himself from the immediate scene of the narration. Didi remained in this position, within hearing of the story, as it unfolded. When his father said that it was unclear to him whether Didi took the initiative to loan his pants to his classmate or whether the teacher borrowed Didi's pants on behalf of the classmate, Didi showed again that he

TABLE 8

FREQUENCIES AND PROPORTIONS OF CHILDREN'S LISTENING IN THE BYSTANDER ROLE
(TAIPEI/LONGWOOD)

Age	Baseline	Listening
2,6	57/55	21(.37)/09(.16)
3,0	81/54	29(.36)/14(.26)
3,6	64/48	29(.45)/12(.25)
4,0	76/23	36(.47)/05(.22)
Total	278/180	115(.41)/40(.22)

was listening. He stepped out of his hiding place and set the record straight, "It's the teacher, it's the teacher who loaned the pants."

Again, intercoder reliability estimates were calculated following the procedures described in Chapter III. These ranged from 0.90 to 1.00 with a mean of 0.96 for Taipei and from 0.92 to 1.00 with a mean of 0.98 for Longwood.

Results are presented in Table 8. The Taipei children engaged in twice as much listening within the bystander role compared with their Longwood counterparts. This pattern applied overall (Taipei: 0.41 vs. Longwood: 0.22) and at every age except 3,0, when the difference favoring Taipei was not as strong. Thus, the Taipei children were more active than the Longwood children within the bystander role. Looking across the age range, the pattern is one of stability in rates of listening, with slightly more listening at 4,0 than at 2,6 in both groups.

DISCUSSION

Like the previous chapter, the results of this chapter point to a complex pattern of similarities and differences between the Taipei and Longwood families. All of the children had daily access to two participant roles, and all engaged actively in both roles at each age, with increases in specific types of active participation as they got older. Both groups of children were more active as initiators of co-narrated stories than they were as authors, resisters, or questioners. And both groups authored more stories as they got older— the clearest indication that they were coming to exercise more control over the narration of their own experience. In addition, as bystanders all of the children sometimes listened to stories.

Differences in Participant Roles

One of the most striking differences was that the Taipei and Longwood families diverged in which participant role they privileged. The Taipei children experienced more stories from the vantage point of the bystander role, whereas the Longwood children experienced more stories from the vantage point of the co-narrator role. This led us to wonder whether each group had an advantage with respect to the participant role that occurred more frequently. In other words, did the Taipei children look more active as bystanders, the Longwood children as co-narrators?

The answer to this question is a resounding "yes" for the bystander role. The rates of listening were twice as high for the Taipei children (who were bystanders to a total of 278 stories) as for the Longwood children (who were bystanders to 98 fewer stories). Moreover, the Taipei children showed signs of listening to one-third of the stories at 2,6 and half of the stories at 4,0. The Longwood children experienced a steady decline across time in the frequency of the bystander role, and their rate of listening never reached one-third. Thus, the difference in sheer frequency favoring the Taipei children was magnified by the differential rates of listening within the bystander role. By both narrating and listening, the Taipei children accrued more narrative experience than their Longwood counterparts.

The pattern with respect to the co-narrator role was not as straightforward, perhaps reflecting the fact that Longwood's frequency advantage was less marked for the co-narrator role (48 more co-narrations for Longwood than for Taipei) than Taipei's was for the bystander role. Overall, the Longwood children did *not* participate more actively than the Taipei children within the co-narrator role. However, their rates of initiating and authoring stories were higher at the younger ages, compared with the Taipei children. This suggests that the co-narrator role may have been more robust very early in development in Longwood. By 4,0, even though most of the Longwood children's experience of personal storytelling took the form of co-narrations, they exceeded their Taipei counterparts on a single type of low-frequency active participation—using questions to express curiosity or seek information or clarification.

The most puzzling finding is that the Longwood children declined dramatically across the age range in their rates of story initiation; at 4,0, they initiated only 0.10 of the co-narrations. Does this mean that the Longwood children's engagement in personal storytelling waned over time? We think not, as there are many ways in which children can be actively engaged. At 4,0, the Longwood children and their co-narrators produced markedly longer stories than they had at the earlier ages (see Chapter III). (Their stories at 4,0 were also longer than the Taipei stories at 4,0.) Thus, the fact that the Longwood 4-year-olds initiated fewer stories but participated in longer stories suggests that they continued to participate actively in personal storytelling. In light of the inherently social nature of personal storytelling, it should also be noted that patterns of initiation and length may also reflect the focal child's adaptation to the changing configurations and contributions of his or her storytelling partners. As presented in Chapter II, each focal child in Longwood had two siblings; as everyone grew older, the focal child might have been encouraged to defer to a younger sibling's attempts to initiate stories. Alternatively, the focal child might have had to vie for the floor among increasingly competitive older siblings. Still another possibility is that the length of stories increased along with the number of story participants, reflecting an increase in the focal child's friendship network.

Meanings of These Socializing Patterns

These patterns of child participation in personal storytelling raise the question of what the co-narrator and bystander roles mean within the two cultural sites. Again, it is important to keep in mind that these are *social* patterns, produced in conjunction with parents, siblings, and others who initiated, elaborated, and sustained them day after day. Parents in both Taipei and Longwood treated very young children as conversational partners, capable of co-narrating their own experience. Although most developmental research takes this cultural assumption for granted, studies of language socialization and other cross-cultural studies have demonstrated that parents from some cultural groups do not treat very young children as conversational partners (Gaskins, 1999; LeVine et al., 1994; Ochs & Schieffelin, 1984). Thus, when Taipei and Longwood are situated within the larger cross-cultural universe, it is possible to tease out a common thread of meaning underlying the routine support of children as co-narrators. Moreover, like many other studies of co-narrations in North American and Chinese samples, this chapter reveals that the Taipei and Longwood children became more active with age within the co-narrator role (e.g., Fivush & Haden, 2003; Haden, Haine, & Fivush, 1997; McCabe, 1997; Miller & Sperry, 1988; Nelson, 1996; Wiley, Rose, Bruner, & Miller, 1998). By the time they were 4 years old, they had amassed an enormous amount of experience of the co-narrator role and were able to take a more active part by initiating, authoring, questioning, and resisting.

The more intriguing finding has to do with what happened in the bystander role, a role that has been studied far less than the co-narrator role. Unlike co-narrations, in which the child is first and foremost a speaker or narrator, this configuration positions the child as a potential listener to another person's rendition of the child's experience. The Taipei children not only occupied the bystander role much more often than the Longwood children, but they also engaged in twice as much listening throughout the age range. This pattern suggests that the Taipei parents and children constructed child listening not as an immature stance appropriate only for 2-year-olds but as a participant role of enduring value, worthy of continuing cultivation (Fung et al., 2004). This interpretation jibes nicely with Jin Li's research (2002,

73

2003b) on Chinese models of learning, which she argues are rooted in the Confucian tradition, and with studies that report a positive association between listening and such qualities as maturity, respect, understanding, and sympathy in Chinese cultures (Gao, 1998; He, 2001; Li, 2009; Yum, 1991). Similarly, in Korea, listening is regarded as a desired skill rather than a deficiency (Kim, 2002) and "thoughtful silence" is the mark of a good student (Kim & Markus, 2002).

Looking beyond Taiwan and its east Asian neighbors, positive cultural stance toward listening was documented three decades ago by Harkness and Super (1977) in Western Kenya and by Greenfield and colleagues (Childs & Greenfield, 1980; Greenfield, 1984) in a Zinacantec Mayan community in Mexico, although these studies did not focus on narrative. Harkness and Super (1977) found that in western Kenya, the Kipsigis people believed that the most important language skill for young children is comprehension, not production, which is congruent with the high value placed on obedience and respect. Similarly, Greenfield and colleagues' research on the teaching of weaving found that Zinacantec Maya learners listened more than they spoke and observed more than they participated (Childs & Greenfield, 1980; Greenfield, 1984). This is part of a larger cultural framework that emphasized the *abnkilal/itzi'nal* (senior/junior) relationship whereby the junior respects the senior. Learning marked by listening, observing, and modeling what the teacher has demonstrated without a process of trial-and-error is also compatible with the cultural ideal of maintaining Zinacanteco tradition, the "true" way (Greenfield & Childs, 1991).

These studies anticipated the recent surge of interest in observing and listening as modes of everyday learning available to children in small-scale agricultural societies (Gaskins & Paradise, 2010). In a far-reaching review paper, Rogoff, Paradise, Arauz, Correa-Chavez, and Angelillo (2003) distinguished between this type of learning, which they dubbed "intent participation," and "assembly-line instruction," in which children are segregated from adult activity and learn via formal education and specialized child-focused instruction in preparation for later admission into adult settings. Two key features of intent participation identified by Rogoff et al. (2003) are relevant to our findings on narrative. The first is that the child deploys his attention actively, and on his own initiative, listening and observing keenly in the bystander role. This active stance seems very compatible with the Taipei children's behavior in the bystander role; even at 2,6, they listened in frequently and without adult encouragement or structuring. The second feature is that children's third-party observation and listening occurs *in anticipation of* their participation in adult activity. In other words, intent participation implies movement from legitimate peripheral participation to central participation (Lave & Wenger, 1991).

Applied to narrative, this second idea suggests that a novice who cannot yet tell a story would first participate peripherally by listening in; once she has learned a lot about storytelling from listening in, she would then step into the more "central" participatory mode of (co) telling the story. It is likely that both the Longwood and Taipei children listened in to stories when they were infants and toddlers, raising the possibility that movement from peripheral to central participation predated our observations. However, we found that the children were already participating frequently as co-narrators at 2,6— a pattern that was especially marked for the Longwood children—*and* they were listening in as bystanders. This raises the possibility that listening in and co-narrating coexisted prior to our first observation.

In any case, the children were still very much novices at 2,6. If they were following the peripheral to central participation model over the span of our observations, we would expect to see an increase in the frequency and sophistication of their participation in co-narrations, with a corresponding decrease in their engagement in listening as bystanders. However, our findings do not support this trajectory in either cultural case. Although listening as bystander predominated in Taipei, and co-narrating predominated in Longwood, these patterns were more or less stable across the age range within each group, a period during which the children did, indeed, become more active and sophisticated co-narrators. In other words, listening from the vantage point of the bystander role did not wane as the children advanced as co-narrators. It thus seems more accurate to think of the bystander/listener role and the co-narrator role not as temporally ordered—with peripheral participation giving way to central participation—but rather as coexisting routes by which children learned to participate in storytelling. After all, mature participation in narrative, whether in Longwood or Taipei, requires facility as both narrator and listener. Apparently, there is room within these roles for cultures to prioritize one over the other and yet maintain this essential reciprocity.

In sum, our findings about participant roles add another layer to the emerging picture of how narrative was practiced with young children in Taipei and Longwood. Although the children had steady access to both bystander/listener and co-narrator roles and became more active participants over the age range, the Taipei families privileged listening and the Longwood families privileged co-narrating.

In Chapter I, we raised the question of how interpretive frameworks and participant roles fit together in the formation of socializing pathways. When viewed in conjunction with the results of Chapter III, the results of this chapter point to a convergence of meaning between the didactic interpretive framework and the privileging of listening in the Taipei stories. As a routine practice, personal storytelling was the site of repeated intersections of Confucian-inflected meaning in which children participated as keenly listening students in relation to their parents as moral authorities and devoted teachers who assiduously guided and corrected them. There was a different but analogous convergence in the Longwood families: The privileging of the co-narrator role went hand-in-hand with narrative interpretations that erased or downplayed the unflattering, accentuated the positive, accepted children's preferences however odd, and encouraged humor. Longwood's version of personal storytelling indexed elements of a childrearing ideology with different goals: fostering children's self-esteem, encouraging the expression of individual preferences and strengths, and helping children to realize their potential (Harwood, Miller, & Irizarry, 1995; Miller et al., 2001, Miller et al., 2002; Shweder et al., 2006; Wiley et al., 1998). In co-narrations of children's past experiences, parents acted as psychological guardians and appreciative audiences, creating protected spaces in which children could voice their preferences, express their good qualities, and craft positive self-images. In the next chapter, we examine how the Taipei and Longwood children navigated stories and made meaning over time within these alternative socializing pathways.

V. CHILDREN NAVIGATING STORIES

Peggy J. Miller, Shumin Lin, Eva Chian-Hui Chen, and Heidi Fung

"Why didn't you reason with me nicely?" (Angu, 4,0)

"Why do you always say I do wonderful things?" (Patrick, 4,0)

As reported in the preceding chapter, the Taipei and Longwood children participated more actively within their respective socializing pathways as they got older. In this chapter, we explore their activeness in more depth. In keeping with the theoretical perspective outlined in Chapter I, our goal here is to bring the children's perspectives into sharper focus. We examine how particular children engaged with stories over time, asking two questions: How did individual children navigate these different versions of personal storytelling? And how did their meaning making change over time within these alternative pathways?

Like other scholars who have studied children's navigation of discursive practices over time (Briggs, 1992, 1998; Corsaro, Molinari, & Rosier, 2002; Michaels, 1991; Miller et al., 1993), we conducted micro-level analysis of transcribed stories to answer these questions. We followed in the interpretive footsteps of the child (Briggs, 1998), attending to the preceding and following interactional contexts in which the narration was embedded as well as details of the content and form of the narrative talk as it unfolded. We inferred the meanings that the focal children and other participants conveyed by tracking who said what to whom and in what manner, including gestures and paralinguistic markings of affect. This approach captures the "choreography of language" (Ochs, 1991). We also paid attention to the larger context of the whole observational session to determine whether and how stories were repeated or occurred in higher order sequences, drawing upon other information about the family, based on field notes and earlier observations.

In choosing which stories to analyze, we were guided by several considerations. We chose stories that exemplified the Taipei and Longwood versions of personal storytelling, as established in Chapters III and IV, and that illustrated changes over time. In each cultural case, the analyses are organized longitudinally in an "overlapping" pattern that featured a few children at each age and followed one of those children at the next age. For example, we focused on Yoyo and Meimei at 2,6, followed Meimei at 3,0 and added Didi at 3,0. At 4,0 ,we featured the child who was the most advanced narrator for her group: Angu and Karen. This strategy captured continuity over time for particular children while also displaying individual variation.

Throughout this chapter, we quote extensively from the transcribed stories. We present the stories primarily in the form of excerpts from transcripts; as in Chapters III and IV, these are set apart from the text in numbered examples. We supplement these transcribed examples with other examples, rendered as prose descriptions. These enrich the description of the children's narrative experience without lengthening the chapter unduly. The chapter is organized as follows: the Taipei children, then the Longwood children, followed by a discussion of the findings.

TAIPEI CHILDREN NAVIGATING STORIES OVER TIME

As reported in Chapter III, many of the Taipei stories revolved around the children's past misdeeds. This chapter will show that some transgression stories were told again and again. As the Taipei children grew older, they exhibited increasingly complex moral reasoning in the co-narrator role. At the same time, they continued to listen attentively as bystanders, sometimes resisting at the older ages.

Two and a Half Years Old: The Baseline

At the earliest age, the Taipei children participated actively but minimally in co-narrating their experience. They followed along with narrations that were structured primarily by older, more competent narrators. Caregivers and siblings structured the stories so as to focus the child's attention on the misdeed: They stated what the child had done wrong, pointed out its consequences, and rehearsed how such situations should be handled in the future. In addition, a key feature of these transgression stories was the repetition of particular stories.

As a baseline example, we begin with a co-narration involving Yoyo and his grandmother (Miller et al., 1997). She initiated the story about two interlinked misdeeds that Yoyo committed earlier in the day: He pushed down a screen, imperiling a vase of flowers, and then objected when his mother punished him. As his grandmother launched the story, she pulled Yoyo closer and held him in her arms. She focused her didactic efforts on Yoyo's response to having committed the misdeed—namely, that he said "don't hit me" when his mother spanked him, which itself constituted a misdeed from his mother's and grandmother's perspectives. She patiently reviewed the incident, pointing out where he went wrong and rehearsing with him what he should have said to his mother after knocking down the screen. She explained that if he admits his misdeeds in the future, his mother will not spank him.

Example 1: Yoyo (2,6) knocked down a screen and then objected when punished

Grandma: Oh, yes, this morning, when Mom was spanking you, what did you say? You said, "Don't hit me," right? Then, what did Grandma tell you to say?

Child: (Quietly) "I won't push the screen down [again]"

Grandma: (Lowers her head and puts her ear next to Yoyo's mouth) Oh right. What would you say to your mom?

Child: I would say to Mom, "I won't push the screen down." (Raises his head and speaks in a very low voice into Grandmother's ear)

Grandma: Oh, you would say to Mom, "Mama, I won't push the screen down [again]," oh?

Child: Hmn (nods).

Grandma: So, Mom wouldn't hit you. Right, oh? If you asked Mom, "You don't hit me," Mom would hit you, right?

Child: Right (nods).

Grandma: So you would directly say to Mom in this way, "Mom, I won't push the screen down." Then how would Mom have reacted?

Child: Won't hit (almost unintelligible).

Grandma: What? (Lowers her head and expects him to speak louder)

Child: Won't hit (quietly).

Grandma: Then she wouldn't hit you, right? Next time when Mom is going to spank you, which sentence is better for you to say to her?

Child: Hmn. Hmn. Say, "I won't push the screen down." (Raises his head and talks into Grandma's ear)

Grandma: Oh, yes. Now you have choices. You say, "Mom, I won't push the screen down." In that way, Mom won't spank you. So next time when Mom is spanking you, you shouldn't say, "You don't hit me (raises her voice and stamps on the floor with her right foot). You don't hit me (raises her voice and stamps on the floor again)." You shouldn't talk that way.

Researcher: (Laughs)

Grandma: [If] you say, "Don't hit me (raises her voice and stamps on the floor)," Mom would even hit more (gently hits Yoyo's butt). Right? Instead, [if] you say to Mom, "I won't push the screen down." What would mom do to you?

Child: (Silently bends forward) "[She will give me] a tender touch." (in Taiwanese, almost unintelligible).

Grandma: What?

Child: "A tender touch." (in Taiwanese)
Grandma: "A tender touch." Ah, she would give you "a tender touch."
           (Both times in Taiwanese) Ah. (Laughs loudly, picks up Yoyo,
           sits him on her lap, and holds him tightly)

Yoyo's grandmother used a series of questions to prompt him to recount how he should have responded when his mother spanked him. This structure allowed Yoyo to participate appropriately while saying very little. Apparently satisfied that Yoyo understood her explanations, she then embarked on an extended rehearsal, invoking hypothetical and future scenarios. Without ever urging Yoyo to listen, she seemed to assume that he would pay attention to her words and be able to follow her complex line of moral reasoning, with rapid shifts in temporal and spatial reference (Fung & Chen, 2001). She also seemed to trust his ability to exercise sound moral judgment in the future.

Throughout this interaction, Yoyo maintained an attentive posture. He answered every prompt appropriately by citing and repeating his grand-mother's words and by nodding, indicating assent to what she was saying. Toward the end of the episode, he came up with a novel contribution that surprised and delighted his grandmother. When Yoyo anticipated that his mother will give him "a tender touch" when he behaves well in the future, he showed that he had listened and comprehended the gist of his grandmother's lesson and was able to project a better self, one that will win his mother's love.

This co-narration was the last in a series of five thematically linked retellings of the "same" events (Fung et al., 2004). This series unfolded over the course of an hour and a half and involved Yoyo, his grandmother, and his older brother. It is thus striking how much time and energy this family spent reviewing these two misdeeds. It is also striking that Yoyo accepted these critiques with patient forbearance, even when his older brother joined in. Yoyo listened attentively, admitted to his transgressions, rehearsed rules of conduct, and imagined doing better in the future. The retellings varied in subtle ways, calling upon Yoyo to pay attention and respond to slightly differ-ent moral implications, even when the "same" event was recounted. Notably, these transgression stories were narrated in a loving manner. For example, in the final retelling, Yoyo's grandmother showed her care and affection with her body language (i.e., holding him close to her, sitting him on her lap, and holding him tightly). This raises the possibility that the intertwining of expressions of love with discourses of moral scrutiny and evaluation may have allowed Yoyo to "hear" critiques without rebelling or becoming discouraged.

Like Yoyo, Meimei, followed along the path that adult co-narrators high-lighted for her, and responded appropriately to their moral guidance. How-ever, most of her narrative experience at 2,6 occurred from the standpoint of the bystander role. In fact, she experienced the most bystander stories of all the Taipei children. In one instance, Meimei's mother told the researcher that Meimei often misplaced her toys, a bad habit that made her mad [*qi si le*]. She went on to relate that she created a "treasure drawer" as a way of dealing with Meimei's annoying habit. She would stash Meimei's mislaid items in the drawer and then Meimei could go to the drawer to retrieve them. As this story unfolded across nine turns, Meimei opened and closed the treasure drawer and then took a toy from the drawer and put it into her pocket. However, the most interesting response occurred after her mother's story ended. Without preamble, Meimei addressed her mother, invoking the rule that applied to the toy: "Cannot go outdoors again." At the same time, she took the toy from her pocket and put it back into the drawer. Having followed the rule, she then teased her mother by pointing at her mother, smiling, and saying, "You're in trouble [*zao gao le*]!" The two then continued to tease each other about getting into trouble. Thus, by voicing a rule at the close of the story, Meimei extended, without prompting, the moral frame of the preceding story, adding, in effect, a moral coda. Like the Yoyo example, this example ended on a light note.

In sum, Yoyo and Meimei illustrate the kind of narrative experiences that were common among the Taipei children at 2,6. Caregivers structured children's participation so that they could contribute nonverbally or with simple utterances. By initiating certain kinds of topics and inviting certain kinds of responses, family members highlighted for them what was worthy of narration: their transgressions and the moral dimensions of their experience. After listening to her mother's story, Meimei displayed that she knew how to behave correctly. Yoyo responded attentively to his grandmother's review of his past misdeeds, even when the same event was narrated again and again. For these families, the past misdeeds of very young children required assiduous attention, but vigilance could be leavened with affection and humor.

Three Years Old

At 3,0 Meimei's family continued to direct her attention to her own misdeeds, and she continued to follow along as others supplied much of the narrative structuring. However, Meimei exhibited more initiative in introducing stories and resisting others' versions of events. The following excerpt comes from a co-narration totaling 49 turns of talk.

Example 2: Meimei (3,0) cut her finger

Child:	(Looks at her own hands and holds up her bandaged finger to show her mother) Mommy, this finger was bleeding.
Mother:	How come it was bleeding?
Child:	(Holds up her finger and walks closer to her mother) Mommy, this finger was bleeding.

Mother:	(Unintelligible)
Child:	(Holds up her finger to her mother and speaks louder) Mommy, this finger was bleeding.
Mother:	(Extends her hands to hold Meimei's hands and looks at Meimei's extended finger) Right, it was bleeding. How come it was bleeding? You tell us!
Researcher:	[to Meimei] What happened [to your finger]?
Mother:	[to Meimei] You tell us!
	(The co-narration continued in this vein for another 16 turns, with Meimei steadfastly maintaining her silence. Finally, Meimei responded.)
Child:	I don't know.
Mother:	How come you don't know? What did you search for in the trash can?
Child:	Search for.
Mother:	Huh?
Child:	Search for the top of the can [the sharp metal top from a can of milk powder].
Mother:	(Walks to the sofa, pulls Meimei to her, and holds up Meimei's hands) Searched for the metal top, right?
Child:	Right.
Mother:	How did the metal top cut your hand?
Child:	Trash can (Unintelligible). (While Meimei talks, she points to her mother, looks at Researcher with an expression of embarrassment and then lowers her voice, making the latter part of her utterance unintelligible)
Mother:	Did it [your finger] bleed? Ah?
Child:	Yes. (Looks embarrassed and buries her face in her mother's lap)
Mother:	(Swats Meimei's bottom twice and then helps Meimei to stand up)
Researcher:	(Laughs) Search for a metal top? What kind of metal top?
Mother:	She is not amenable to discipline [*guan*]. She, that, milk powder, I had opened the metal top of the milk powder can, [I] threw it away to the trash can and [she] ran to search for it. Once she found it, it cut her hand.
Child:	(Stands straight next to her mother, looks embarrassed)
Researcher:	Oh! That really hurts. It makes [you] bleed!
Mother:	[to Meimei] Did it hurt? Did it hurt?

This co-narration continued for several more turns in which Meimei emphasized that she did not cry when she cut her finger. The story ended with her mother expressing her affection and concern for Meimei, "Luckily, luckily, it didn't cut too deep."

Although Example 2 touches on many potential meanings that could have been developed, Meimei's mother crafted a cautionary tale: Meimei misbehaved, and as a result, cut her finger. Meimei responded with silence to her mother's version. However, her mother persisted until Meimei supplied an acceptable response. From that point onwards, Meimei acceded to her mother's rendition. Thus, within the course of a single narrative Meimei displayed her versatility as initiator, resister, and reluctant collaborator.

At the same age, Didi and his family told a series of co-narrated and bystander stories about his experiences of fighting in which they constructed, negotiated, and contested rules and their moral implications. While Didi's fights with his sister were always negatively evaluated by his parents, his fights at school presented moral ambiguities that the family pondered. In the following co-narrated story about an event in which Didi fought with a classmate, Didi first had to contend with his sister, who positioned herself as a witness to the event.

Example 3: Didi (3,0) fought with his classmate

Mother:	Didn't you have a fight with Kiki?
Child:	Yes.
Sister.	Yeah. He often fought at school. I asked him not to fight.
Mother:	And? Who won the fight?
Child:	I don't know.
Sister:	They both lost.
Researcher:	Who is Kiki?
Father:	Kiki is a classmate.
Mother:	Oh, so Didi lost, right?
Child:	No (shakes head). Kiki lost. I won.
Sister:	He lies every time.
Mother:	(Laughs)
Sister:	I saw with my own eyes that he was beaten and cried.
Child:	I didn't.
Sister:	And he went to report to the teacher.
Child:	I didn't.
Sister:	The teacher even scolded you. And you dare say you didn't?!
Child:	No, the teacher did not scold me. (Co-narration continues).

In the first part of this co-narration Didi defended his version of the fight against the resolute opposition of his older sister, who portrayed Didi as a fighter, a loser, a liar, and a tattletale! A few turns later, however, the story took a different turn when Didi's mother criticized him for his role in the fight ("Don't fight to grab the round [Lego blocks]. Everyone can play. There is no need to fight.") Surprisingly, Didi's sister then defended him and blamed Kiki for starting the fight, and Didi offered his own defense ("There were no round shapes left [after Kiki took all of them]."). In the end, Didi's mother and father also sided with Didi against Kiki.

Later in the taping session, when his sister was out of the living room, Didi retold the story of his fight with Kiki. But when he saw his sister emerge from a nearby bedroom, he brought the story to a halt, "I don't want to talk about it!" This series of fight stories illustrates Didi's investment in justifying his behavior when in morally dubious situations and his skill at evading narrations in which his version of the event might be challenged.

At the same age, Didi continued to participate in storytelling as a bystander, listening, mostly without protest, as family members presented him as a transgressor in past events (e.g., not putting his toys away, being easily frightened, and crying inappropriately).

In sum, at 3,0 Meimei and Didi illustrate a more advanced moment in their navigation of the didactic pathway. They were able to do more than follow along: they initiated more stories, offered their own ideas and interpretations, and supplied information that their co-narrators lacked. They also illustrated more complex engagement with moral reasoning. While they continued to listen, as bystanders, as their own experiences were narrated by family members, they were also able to defend themselves and resist other narrators' versions of events.

Three and a Half Years Old

When Didi was 3,6 his family continued to remind him of his past misdeeds (e.g., "He never listens!" "He is a crybaby." "Your cars were all broken, right?"), establishing his propensity to fight as an ongoing theme. Continuing to exhibit keen investment in the kind of moral self that he projected, Didi became even more skilled at justifying his actions and reasoning about wrongdoing. For example, with minimal structuring by co-participants, he related the following story, "I didn't do anything, and then he [a classmate] hit me first. . . .Because he is bad. He scratched my eyes."

When Didi was 3,6 his family devoted even more time to the practice of narrative debriefing, taking up particular instances of Didi's wrongdoing and subjecting them to repeated and prolonged scrutiny. In one such case, the main "facts" of the incident were not in dispute: Didi hit his sister with a ball and made her mouth bleed. Still, mother, older sister, and Didi had a great deal to say about what happened, constructing a series of six related discursive segments: (a) Didi's sister complained that her mouth still hurt; (b) Didi's mother narrated the incident, with Didi and his sister as bystanders; (c) mother, sister, and Didi co-narrated the story; (d) Didi returned to the story; (e) Didi again revisited the story; and (f) Didi's sister told their mother a related story about Didi, casting Didi as bystander. The important point for present purposes is that Didi flexibly and energetically pursued his goals throughout these permutations. He assumed more responsibility than he had in the past for keeping the topic in play, twice initiating a return to the story. Across these several repetitions, he vigorously defended his actions, arguing that because his aim was so accurate, his sister should have taken evasive action to protect herself. Then, he asserted that his sister complained too much about bleeding compared to his own lack of complaint when injured. Later, when his mother produced the usual rule reminder, "So next time, don't hit others with a ball without a reason, OK? Um?" Didi responded with a hasty, "OK. OK," and then challenged the validity of the moral rule that his mother invoked, "Does it matter that I hit others and make them bleed?" His mother responded with consternation, "How can it be possible that it doesn't matter? It's serious! It's terrible that someone bleeds!"

Angu, another focal child, resembled Didi in her nimble responses to family members' narrations both within and across repeated tellings. Angu did not like to take naps at preschool, and her noncompliance became a matter for repeated review. During the 3,6 observation, Angu, her aunt (her primary caregiver), and her school-aged cousin co-narrated an incident in which Angu played with her classmates instead of taking a nap, resulting in punishment by the teacher. Although Angu did not challenge her aunt and cousin's account of her misdeed, she did add mitigating information, stressing that she and her classmate did not cry when the teacher punished them. (Angu's aunt, like the other caregivers in the study regarded crying of this sort as a transgression.) A little while later, the aunt re-narrated this story to the researcher, casting Angu as a bystander. This was followed by still another repetition, a three-way co-narration:

Example 4: Angu (3,6) played during nap time

Aunt:	Did you get up from the bed?
Child:	(Nods her head)
Aunt:	Oh, what did you get up for?
Child:	(In a joyful manner) I got up to play with my classmates. I played!
Researcher:	(Laughs)
Aunt:	So then your classmates did not sleep either?
Child:	Yes. (Nods)
Cousin:	(In a low voice) Others were very much disturbed by your noise. (Seven more turns ensue)
Aunt:	Yes, I think others were very much disturbed by your noise.
Child:	Two other classmates were disturbing others too.

Researcher:	Two other students were woken up by you?
Child:	Their noise disturbed me from sleeping.
Aunt:	What? Your classmates disturbed you?
Child:	(Nods her head)
Aunt:	I don't think so.

In response to her aunt's question, Angu readily and matter-of-factly acknowledged that she broke the naptime rule. She also admitted, with pleasure in her voice that she did so in order to play with her classmates. When her aunt and cousin aligned with one another in disapproving of Angu for disturbing the children who were trying to nap, Angu deftly changed her story and blamed two other classmates for disturbing her and preventing her from sleeping.

Another important advance in moral reasoning at 3,6 was a concern with intentionality. For example, Yoyo, initiated a story by saying, "I released two birds yesterday, I was, I was going to play with them." Then he added, "[The birds] were released by me accidentally." When his older brother challenged this interpretation, Yoyo repeated that the birds were released accidentally, and his mother supported Yoyo's claim. Similarly, in a bystander story, Angu's aunt recounted that Angu told her father on the phone that she was "in trouble" because she had broken her cousin's piggy bank. Angu then asked her father, "Daddy, what if, what would happen if I did something wrong by accident? What would happen if I did something wrong on purpose?" This story is especially intriguing in that the aunt represented Angu as taking the initiative to call her father on the phone to consult with him about the moral implications of her misdeed. This example also illustrates a story embedded in a story: the aunt told the researcher a story of how Angu told her father a story of breaking her cousin's piggy bank.

In sum, at age 3,6, Didi, Yoyo, and Angu continued to be highly engaged in casting their past experiences in a moral framework. They became increasingly active moral agents, initiating more moral stories, vigorously pursuing those topics, introducing the issue of intentionality, mitigating their own misdeeds, and even challenging moral rules. They also exhibited increasing interactional agility. Yet, they continued to participate as silent overhearers or listeners when others represented them as transgressors in past events. Moreover, as the children's verbal skills improved, it became apparent that they varied among themselves in the ways in which they took up the morally saturated discourses at hand. With his proclivity for conflict and fighting, Didi was called a "rascal" by his parents. He became adept at defending himself and was more likely than the other focal children to discredit and blame others. Yoyo, on the other hand, reflected on his own misdeeds with quiet intensity, a posture that was already evident at 2,6 (Example 1), and Angu stood out for her emotional expressiveness and verbal precocity.

Four Years Old

At the oldest age, the Taipei children were able to hold their own as narrators, taking a substantial role in steering the conversation toward the kinds of narratable topics and interpretive frames prompted and modeled earlier by their mothers and other more competent narrators. The children used these frames to reflect on their own past experiences. They used the moral standards upheld by adults to judge their own and others' behavior. In addition to narrating their misdeeds, they began to treat *not* transgressing as a reportable event. In other words, they told stories about situations in which they did not engage in misdeeds for which they had been scolded in the past. For example, Yoyo told the researcher, "We did not fight today!" and then he and his brother co-narrated why they did not fight.

The children also used invidious comparisons as a way of extolling their own virtuous conduct. However, Angu, the most sophisticated narrator among the Taipei children was the only child who used this strategy to judge adults. In the conversation preceding the following narration, the researcher asked Angu's aunt, who was Protestant and regularly took Angu to church, whether Angu's mother was also Protestant. Angu jumped into the conversation, initiating a story in which she adopted the voice of religious authority against her parents.

Example 5: Angu (4,0) judged her parents' religious practice

Child:	My mother worshipped Buddhist gods.
Aunt:	Really, that's not good.
Child:	(Loudly) Right, that's bad! (Short digression)
Researcher:	Does her father worship Buddhist gods?
Aunt:	Yes, he worshipped a lot.
Child:	He did. I did not. (Aunt and Researcher both laugh)
Child:	Worshipping Buddhist gods is not good.
Researcher:	Oh.
Child:	Worshipping Buddhist gods is the worst!
Aunt:	Oh.
Child:	My father worshipped Buddhist gods, a lot! Wherever he saw [temples], he worshipped.
Aunt:	(Laughs) Oh, my. Really. He is infamous. I don't know how he can clear his name.
Child:	He brought me to worship gods, and I didn't want to.
Aunt:	(Laughs) Miss, are you having a religious revolution?

This story illustrates how Angu seized the opportunity to steer the conversation in a morally evaluative direction. She revealed to her aunt and the researcher that her mother worshipped Buddhist gods, which elicited a critical comment from her aunt. Angu then went on to criticize her father for the same bad behavior, distinguishing herself so emphatically ("He did. I did not.") that her interlocutors burst into laughter. She further condemned her parents' behavior, simultaneously presenting herself as morally superior by stating that she refused to worship Buddhist gods with her father. Her aunt responded to her niece's increasingly extreme condemnations with laughter and commented with amusement on her vehemence.

The following narration concerning Angu's transgression on the morning of her birthday illustrates her strong resistance and cleverness in avoiding an undesired topic. Angu's aunt initiated the story by urging Angu to tell the researcher what happened. The story that the aunt was trying to elicit was that Angu was running and knocked into a plate, causing food to spill; her aunt spanked her for her carelessness.

Example 6: Angu (4,0) resisted telling what she did wrong on her birthday

Aunt:	(Unfriendly tone) How did you spend your birthday?
Researcher:	Oh, yes.
Child:	(Sits on a chair quietly, smiles at Researcher and Aunt)
Researcher:	How did you spend your birthday?
Aunt:	How did you spend your birthday?
Child:	(Looks at Researcher with a smile)
Researcher:	Wow, how come you do not talk?
Aunt:	So after being punished, you become dumb.

In this initial segment of the interaction, the aunt tried again and again to extract the story from Angu, with occasional comments and prompts from the researcher, but Angu did not accede to her aunt's demand. This pattern continued for 20 more turns, with Angu repeatedly refusing to narrate the misdeed. She repeatedly said, "I don't want to tell" and "I'm embarrassed to tell." She then put her head on her arm, laughed, and hid her face. As her aunt and the researcher continued to press her, she tried to change the topic and succeeded in creating a temporary digression. When her aunt returned to the topic, Angu gave in at last:

Example 6:(continued) Angu (4,0) gave in and told what she did wrong

Child:	(In a low voice) I tell you one thing. Auntie hit me on my birthday morning.
Researcher:	(Laughs) Why? There must be a reason.
Child:	(Whispers) Because I kicked a plate flying away.
Researcher:	You what?
Child:	(A bit louder) I kicked a plate flying far away!
	(Angu changes the topic to the fun activities on her birthday)

This part of the narration shows that under duress, Angu eventually confessed, but she did so reluctantly, whispering a very brief account to the researcher. The manner in which she delivered this sub-rosa communication raises the question of whether Angu intended to confess or to accuse her aunt and whether she expected to find a more sympathetic audience in the researcher. Altogether, this tense co-narration lasted for 10 min, and during that time, Angu used various clever maneuvers to subvert her aunt's goal: silence, explicit refusals to tell, displays of embarrassment, creation of a diversion, a brief, ambiguous confession/accusation, and finally a successful attempt to steer the story to the fun activities on her birthday.

Later in the taping session, Angu returned to this story, taking her aunt to task for being too severe in her discipline. This co-narration was preceded by a debate between her and her aunt about who was the noisiest. Angu teasingly said that her aunt was the noisiest and the aunt retorted, "It is you who likes to fight. I never fight with you!" At this point, Angu returned to the story of her transgression on the morning of her birthday. Frustrated and angry with her aunt, who had been tired and less patient than usual during this observation session (Fung et al., 2004), Angu brought her formidable moral reasoning powers to bear.

Example 7: Angu (4,0) criticized her aunt for being too severe in her discipline

Child:	Why didn't you reason with me nicely?
Aunt:	Yes, why didn't you reason with me nicely?
Child:	(Raises her voice and points at her aunt) I say you! (Emphatically)
Aunt:	I say you. You should have talked to me nicely.
Child:	(Points at Aunt) So should you!
Aunt:	(Jokingly) Then you, it's you who picked a fight!
Child:	(Points at Aunt) Mama, I'm asking you a question, when I kicked the dishes, kicked [them] far away, why were you unreasonable to me? Tell me. (Holds up her chin with a scornful expression) Hum!
Aunt:	In what way was I unreasonable? You knocked over my dishes, "ping ping pang," that far. You kicked it all the way, kicked "ping pang" that far. What did you do? Early in the morning, you kicked dishes, from that....How come you didn't walk carefully but instead rushed into all those dishes, which were all broken by your kick?
Child:	Because I fell! (Very loudly)
Aunt:	Why did you fall? How come you didn't know how to walk? (Looks down and talks to the baby sister who is drinking milk in her arms) Your sister is quarreling. Boys, isn't she mad? (Laughs,

	looks up, and talks to Angu again) Why did you [do that], you give me a reason for that.
Child:	Disgusting! (Loudly)
Aunt:	Huh? Right? Why everyday you cannot (interrupted by Angu)
Child:	Not right! (Loudly)
Aunt:	Why can't you ever sit properly when you eat? And, then, whatever you eat [or drink], you spill. Whatever you eat, you spill.
Child:	(In a very serious tone) But why didn't you reason with me nicely? It's not that you didn't have Daddy and Mommy. You had Daddy and Mommy before. When you were young, didn't you ever spill?
Aunt:	Me? I was very well-behaved. I never spilled food.
Child:	Really?
Aunt:	Yes.
Child:	Yes?
Aunt:	You ask your mom, ask her whether I spilled my food when I was little.
Child:	I want to ask your grandma.
Aunt:	Right. You want to ask my grandma? No, you ask my mom, your grandma.
Child:	Yes. I will ask her right now.
Aunt:	Ok, you call her and ask.
Child:	Ok.
Aunt:	Ok.
Child:	What's her telephone number?
Child:	(Goes to the phone and tries to call her grandmother, but her grandmother is not at home).

In this remarkable co-narration, Angu displayed the full scope of her moral and narrative sophistication. First, in the midst of her teasing exchange with her aunt, Angu redirected the conversation to the story in question, going directly to the heart of the matter, "Why didn't you reason with me nicely?" Second, instead of construing her own past behavior from her aunt's perspective (i.e., as a rule infraction), Angu turned the tables, judging her aunt to be in the wrong. Third, Angu forcefully challenged her aunt's moral reasoning, claiming that she had broken the dishes accidentally, not deliberately. Then Angu went on to muster another powerful argument against her aunt: She reasoned that children always spill and that her aunt, as a child, had been no different! When her aunt denied this, Angu went to the phone and called her aunt's mother. Although Angu's aunt did not cede any ground throughout this exchange, it is important to note the she tolerated Angu's onslaught and did not silence or punish her for speaking her mind.

At this age, Angu also participated in narrative practices as bystander, sometimes quietly listening without protest, but sometimes turning herself from a bystander into a co-narrator to present herself in a morally positive light. For example, when her aunt complained to the researcher that Angu always spilled food or drinks, Angu first listened attentively and then she initiated a story in which her cousin gave her ice cream and soda when her aunt was not at home and proudly claimed, "I did not spill!"

In sum, these examples of Angu's stories illustrate what is possible at age 4 when an emotionally expressive, verbally advanced child engages deeply and repeatedly in didactic narrative practices. Although Angu and the other children showed an emerging ability at 3,6 to voice their own moral perspectives, by 4,0 Angu had advanced much farther, displaying a precocious level of moral autonomy.

LONGWOOD CHILDREN NAVIGATING STORIES OVER TIME

In parallel with the previous section, here we follow the Longwood children as they navigate the child-affirming pathway. It is important to note that the increasingly complex moral reasoning that the Taipei children exhibited in the narrative context did not occur for the Longwood children. As reported in Chapter III, the Longwood stories rarely invoked children's misdeeds and thus did not offer a narrative venue for developing a sense of moral problem. However, the Longwood stories did involve other matters of keen abiding interest to the Longwood children. And these children too participated in repeated tellings of particular stories.

Two and a Half Years Old: The Baseline

At the earliest age, the Longwood children, like the Taipei children, participated actively but minimally in narrations of their experience. They followed along as older, more competent speakers structured the narrations for them. However, the content and structuring differed in many ways from the Taipei stories. Consider again Example 1 from Chapter IV. When Tommy's mother initiated the co-narration by saying, "Who was in charge of the salt and pepper?" he replied, "Me." She then asked, "What did you do?" and Tommy made a shaking motion. A few turns later, she asked, "How did we make the potatoes?" Tommy replied, "Um, good" that prompted her to affirm his response ("Oh, we made them good.") and to invite more information ("How did we make them?").

Tommy's mother's use of questions to structure the story allowed Tommy to take an active part in the co-narration while contributing only four brief utterances; his mother further supported his involvement by affirming his responses. At the same time, she articulated the important role that he played in the narrated activity of cooking: She told him that he was "in charge of the salt and pepper," described this as his "job," explained what his job entailed, "You had to shake the salt and pepper all over the potatoes," and finally summed up his role: "He was the cook. He was my helper." In both the narrated event (cooking) and the event of narration (co-narration), Tommy's mother highlighted the competence of her very young son despite his very real limitations as cook and narrator.

In other co-narrations at this age, Tommy's mother drew his attention to his likes and dislikes, initiating one story by saying, "Tommy, how did you like t-ball? What did you do while we were at t-ball? Wanna tell dad?" In another co-narration, she encouraged him to talk about a new food that he enjoyed, "They were so much fun and you loved it," coaching him until he came up with the name, "artichokes." In still another case, Tommy's mother initiated a story about his recent bout of chicken pox, prompting various details, including "Did you like having the chicken pox?" to which he replied, "Nuh huh."

In addition to stories that focused on Tommy's competencies and preferences, this family used humor in rendering Tommy's experiences:

Example 8: Tommy (2,6) was watered and clipped

Mother:	Did you tell dad about Fred? Did you tell him?
Child:	He watered me.
Mother:	He watered him up. You better tell J [Researcher] who Fred is.
Researcher:	Who watered you?
Mother:	She's gonna wonder what we're talking about! (Laughs)
Researcher:	Yeah! (Laughs)
Father:	What did Fred do?
Child:	Um, um, he watered me.
Father:	And then what did he do?
Mother:	What else did he do to you?
Child:	He clipped me.
Mother:	What else did he do?
Father:	What did he clip?
Child:	My hair.

This co-narration continued through six more turns, concluding with the information that Fred was a barber and with more laughter from Tommy's mother and the researcher.

In sum, Tommy and his family illustrate the kind of co-narrative experience that was typical of the Longwood children at the earliest age. Tommy's mother structured his participation so that he could contribute to the narration of his experience through simple verbal utterances, and she affirmed and inflated his contributions. Moreover, by initiating certain kinds of topics and inviting certain kinds of response, Tommy's family highlighted for him what was worthy of narration: His competencies and preferences and the humorous dimensions of his experience. Although Tommy seldom showed signs of listening as a bystander, bystander stories showed the same selective bias: events, activities, books, films, and characters that Tommy liked or disliked, competencies and accomplishments, and funny events.

Three Years Old

At 3,0 the events that Tommy and his family selected to narrate were similar to those described at 2,6. In co-narrated and bystander stories, they continued to talk about his preferences (e.g., "So, he's really into picking out his own clothes these days," "He's really into it [preschool]"). As mentioned in Chapter III, there were several stories featuring Tommy's desire to have a lion costume and the special efforts required to obtain the coveted costume, only to have Tommy declare, once he saw himself in the mirror, "My costume is dumb." This humorous denouement was quoted by Tommy's older sister, his mother, and Tommy himself.

The longest and most highly developed co-narration at this age involved Tommy and his mother, with occasional comments and questions from the researcher. The story began with a series of questions about what happened at a Halloween party and then continued as follows:

Example 9: Tommy (3,0) liked Kelly's costume

(Previous turns)

Mother:	Who were you hanging around with?
Child:	Um, um, um guess who Kelly's sister was, Ellen?
Mother:	Who was, what was she, what was Ellen?
Child:	Um Bo Peep.
Mother:	Little Bo Peep. What was Kelly?
Child:	Um, um pine cone.
Mother:	Oh, pine cone (pause) you wanna know what it real-, what another name for it is?
Child:	Yeah.
Mother:	Unicorn. (Pause) Kelly was a unicorn because she has one horn coming out her nose, right? She was a unicorn.
Child:	She was a unicorn fish!
Mother:	A unicorn fish?
Researcher:	That is a great idea!
Mother:	That was interesting, huh? Did you like her costume?

Child:	Yeah.
Mother:	Which costume did you like the best (pause) at the party?
Child:	Um Kelly's.
Mother:	Oh, you liked Kelly's. How come?
Child:	Because.
Mother:	Just because?
Child:	Because.
Mother:	Because.
Child:	I love Kelly.
Mother:	Oh, I know you do love Kelly . . . . (Co-narration continues)

Compared with the co-narrations at 2,6, this example was not as highly structured by Tommy's mother; Tommy behaved more like a genuine conversational partner, imparting information that his interlocutors lacked. For example, when his mother asked, "Who were you hanging around with?" he did not answer the question, but rather directed a question to her, "Um, um, um guess who Kelly's sister was, Ellen?" As the story unfolded, the content and framing apparent at 2,6 emerged in this story but with Tommy assuming a larger but still limited role in sustaining them. For example, when Tommy's mother very gently corrected his misnomer ("unicorn" instead of "pine cone"), Tommy responded with a spot of humor, "A unicorn fish!" which was immediately affirmed as an original and interesting idea by both the researcher and Tommy's mother. The latter then asked Tommy which costumes he liked, an exchange that led him to acknowledge that he liked Kelly's costume the best and loved Kelly.

The longest co-narration for Amy (3,0), another focal child, showed the same hallmarks. Consisting of almost 60 turns, this co-narration included Amy's mother, her older sister, and the researcher. Amy introduced the topic of Midnight, a horse that she met earlier in the day when the family went to a park. Like Tommy, Amy then contributed information that her mother did not have, "I want name Wakeup," to which her mother replied, "Oh, you named the other horse Wakeup, huh, cause one is Midnight? I understand." The researcher remarked, "That's a good idea," to which Amy's mother replied, "Yeah, she's, she's a good thinker." With this comment, Amy's mother not only agreed with the researcher's compliment but also explicitly interpreted Amy's narrated behavior as evidence of a general cognitive attribute.

The story continued with the several participants establishing that Amy was excited when she saw the horse, that she and her sister ran to it, and petted it. In this part of the story, Amy introduced two story actions ("when we runned to the horse," "and I can't reach it"), without the help of preceding questions. Several turns later, the following exchange ensued:

Example 10: Amy (3,0) enjoyed the horses

Mother:	What part of the horse did you pet, sweetie, do you remember?
Child:	I go down and up, down and up, down and up.
Researcher:	Down and up. What part of him did you pet, down and up, down and up?
Child:	Mm hmm.
Researcher:	Where, what part of him? Where on the horse?
Mother:	At the tummy?
Child:	(Nods)
Researcher:	Yeah?
Mother:	Oh, you fooler.
Child:	Not (pause) on his back.... (Co-narration continues)

This part of the story reveals that there were times when Amy's mother continued to ask structuring questions (which were repeated by the researcher, in this instance) and that she, like Tommy's mother, noticed but downplayed Amy's factual errors, calling her a "fooler."

In sum, at 3,0 Tommy and Amy illustrate a slightly more advanced moment in meaning making. They were able to do more than follow along while more competent narrators carried the weight of the co-narration: They offered their own ideas and interpretations and supplied information that their interlocutors did not have. They also collaborated with parents and siblings in selectively narrating strengths and preferences and elaborating the humorous and positive dimensions of experience. Adults continued to praise and affirm their children and to use humor in response to inaccuracies.

Three and a Half Years Old

At this age, Amy took a more active part in introducing humor. She playfully corrected her mother by saying, "No silly head, at the theater, silly," a comment that echoes the tone of her mother's earlier comment to her, "Oh, you fooler." In another co-narration, the following exchange occurred: Amy's mother asked, "Amy, what do you say sometimes? Instead of 'give me a break,' you say ___?" to which Amy and her older sister replied in unison, "'Yeah, yeah, yeah.'" Amy then said, "'Take a break–Not!'" and her mother responded, "You crack me up, Amy Miloy, you crack me up."

There was also a noticeable increase in the children's narrative competence and ability to exercise control over the story. Example 11 (below) provides a good example but requires attention to the preceding context in order to fully appreciate Amy's narrative competence. This co-narration was preceded by a conversation in which Amy declared, "Police are important," prompting her 5-year-old sister to relate a story about a time that a policeman sat down next to the family at McDonald's and ate his lunch, an event that she and the focal child thought was funny. Amy then initiated a story that furthered the conversational topic:

Example 11: Amy (3,6) related that the CD player was stolen

Child: One time, we go to see Snow White at, at, at the___.
Mother: At the theater?
Child: Yeah, and someone stole something like that from the car.
Mother: Right, and when we came out ___.
Child: The VCR... the CD player [was missing].
Mother: The CD player (gestures thumbs up) excellent! Boy, you see those wheels turning! (Co-narration continues)

In this example, Amy not only took the lead in narrating the details of what happened, but she deftly inserted the story into the ongoing conversation, prefacing the story with the conventional opener, "One time." In an instance of story chaining (see Cho & Miller, 2004), Amy offered her story about the CD player being stolen in response to her sister's prior story about a policeman; in a similar situation, an adult might say, "Speaking of policemen, one time..." In addition, Amy's retrieval of the correct detail (CD player) was greeted with gestural and verbal praise from her mother. As in the earlier example (3,0), in which Amy's mother described her as a "good thinker," here she drew attention to her young daughter's cognitive competence.

In other co-narrations at 3,6, Amy was praised for remembering and for being "a special helper" with household chores. And in a co-narration about missing the Valentine's Day party at school, Amy's mother reminded her that the teachers saved a whole bag of treats for her, adding, "They were so thoughtful. They must like you big time." Similarly, in one of only four bystander stories that occurred at this age, Amy's mother related that Amy had asked an interesting question ("How can we talk?") the day before. This story was occasioned by Amy's repetition of the question during the taping session.

At this same age, Patrick and his family told several stories about his experiences with severe asthma, necessitating hospitalizations and visits to the emergency room. Several of these stories were bystander stories in which his mother portrayed him as handling these scary experiences with aplomb. For example, she related that during a recent hospitalization, Patrick entertained himself in between treatments by playing 30 games on a new board game; Patrick's 6-year-old brother, Mitchell then chimed in, "He loves it [the game]."

However, unlike their mother, Mitchell did not always portray his brother in a positive light. For example, in a bystander story about a trip to the emergency room, Mitchell's contributions consisted of the following: "He turned green in the car.... His whole body turned um green.... Yeah, Patrick is a whiner kid."

Like the other Longwood families, Patrick's family seasoned their stories with humor. In the following co-narration, Patrick and Mitchell joined forces to tease the researcher. Although Mitchell launched this co-narration, it was Patrick who added inventive detail about germs, thereby furthering the humor of this small off-color drama.

Example 12: Patrick (3,6) and his older brother (6,0) as co-teasers

Brother:	Patrick, he always pees in his bed and he peed in his bed just today.
Researcher:	Did you do that, Patrick?
Child:	(Nods and smiles) Went pee-pee in my bed.
Brother:	So, now I go pee in my bed.
Researcher:	Is that funny, that you peed in your bed?
Child:	(Nods and smiles) I said, "Mommy, I got germs all over my bed and I like germs."
Brother:	He did it on purpose.
Researcher:	You like germs (laughs)? What did mom say? What did your mom say?
Child:	(Softer voice) I don't know. (Looks away from Researcher)
Researcher:	Cause you didn't say that to her, did you?
Child:	(Shakes head)
Researcher:	You're making it up.

In this example, Patrick and Mitchell pretended to be babies. They used baby talk (perhaps imitating their baby sister) and claimed to have the kind of mishap that babies are prone to.

In sum, at 3,6 the same selective bias in narratable events and details that was evident at the earlier ages continued to hold sway, with the children taking a still more active role in articulating their strengths and preferences and introducing and sustaining humor. Their interlocutors continued to affirm the children's contributions and to portray them favorably. In addition, patterns of interpretation and attribution that distinguished one child from another were discernible. Whereas Amy's mother saw evidence, in story after story, that her daughter was a good thinker, Patrick's mother repeatedly noticed her son's bravery and equanimity in the face of scary physical symptoms and medical procedures.

Four Years Old

At the oldest age, the children were able to hold their own as narrators, taking a substantial role in steering the conversation toward the kinds of narratable topics modeled earlier by their mothers and other family members. The children appropriated and pondered the child-affirming interpretive frame, using it to construe, quite articulately, their own past experiences.

Example 13: Patrick (4,0) expressed curiosity about his mother's compliment

Sibling:	I a big girl, I a big girl (singing, imitating a song that Patrick just sang).
Mother:	Pat, do you teach Susie all these things?
Child:	(Nods)
Researcher:	That's what big brothers are for, huh?
Mother:	It's one of those wonderful things.
Child:	Why do I do, why do you always say I do wonderful things?
Mother:	Because you're so wonderful.
Child:	Because I always give you flowers?
Mother:	(Smiles and nods)
Researcher:	Do you give your mom flowers?
Child:	Um hum.
Mother:	All the time. (Co-narration continues)
Child:	I take them [the flowers] out.
Researcher:	From where?
Child:	The grass.
Researcher:	Out of the grass?
Mother:	My favorite flower's dandelions (laughs).
Researcher:	Oh yeah? [to Patrick] Wow, that's so thoughtful of you.

This story was occasioned by Patrick's little sister's imitation of him. His mother interpreted Susie's song as evidence that Patrick had taught Susie "all these things," implying that he was a good big brother. Patrick nodded in agreement with this favorable description of himself, which was affirmed by the researcher. Patrick's mother then offered a more explicit compliment, "It's one of those wonderful things," to which Patrick replied, "Why do I do, why do you always say I do wonderful things?" With this expression of curiosity, Patrick succinctly characterized one of the interpretive threads— the child-favorability bias—that ran through his mother's portrayals of him during the entire age range. His mother's response to his question, "Because you're so wonderful," did not satisfy his curiosity, leading him to ask another question, "Because I always give you flowers?"

The next example also illustrates a sophisticated grasp of the favorability bias. But instead of asking questions, Amy enacted this bias, constructing a story around her triumph at day camp.

Example 14: Amy (4,0) and her sister got medals

Researcher:	How was day camp today?
Child:	Great.
Sister:	Good. You know what? I got a real medal.
Researcher:	You got a real medal?
Child:	And I got this one.
Researcher:	Wow, what did you get?
Child:	I got this one.
Sister:	Because we were so good at play camp.
Child:	I got it from, I got it from play camp. (Co-narration continues)
Mother:	What Emily, let me ask Amy a question, what, what day was today? At play camp, what did they call it?
Child:	We had to throw something on a (unintelligible) thing. And they jumped (unintelligible) and one of my counselors and, and, and one of them said, "Wow!"
Mother:	One of them said, "wow," when you jumped? One of your counselors? That's when you were playing, in the uh, cause it was Olympics Day.
Child:	You should have watched!
Mother:	I should have watched? Yeah, I wish I could have been there but I had some work to do . . . . (Co-narration continues)

Although Amy's 6-year-old sister was the first to mention getting a medal at day camp, Amy repeatedly matched her sister's claim. When her mother held the floor for Amy and prompted her to explain that it was Olympics Day at day camp, Amy did not respond as her mother intended. Instead she excitedly related *her* story: She performed so well in the athletic event that her counselor said, "'Wow!'" When her mother affirmed and expanded Amy's story, Amy said, "You should have watched!" From Amy's standpoint, an important element in the drama of her successful performance was the positive evaluation of adults, both her camp counselor, whose praise she quoted and her mother, whom she wished had been there to witness her triumph.

Another interpretive thread that the children had encountered many times before and now used with increased facility was the focus on likes and dislikes. They not only introduced their own preferences but reasoned about them and talked about related subjective experiences. Karen was the most sophisticated Longwood narrator. At 4,0 she participated in several stories concerning her "special blankets." Karen had a history of emotional attachments to blankets and, with parental encouragement, was struggling to relinquish her latest blanket. In the conversational lead-up to the following example, Karen's father proposed teasingly that she give away her blanket to the researcher, prompting Karen to laugh. Eventually, Karen agreed, leading her father to ask, "And then we'll get rid of your blanket forever?" Karen then turned to the researcher and narrated what happened when she tried to give up her blanket:

Example 15: Karen (4,0) dreamt about her blanket

Child: I try to sleep without it now.
Researcher: You're trying to sleep without it?
Child: I, I tried to sleep with [out it], I kept dreaming about it when I, when I was like at my Grandpa Will's cause I didn't have it.
Researcher: Uh, huh.
Child: Kept dreaming about it.
Researcher: Oh, you missed it.
Child: (Laughs) No.

Karen introduced the story to an uninformed interlocutor, and then, without co-narrator assistance, produced several interlinked clauses to convey what happened. Moreover, in reporting that she dreamt about the relinquished blanket, Karen articulated an inner psychological experience that only she could have known about. The co-narrated blanket stories illustrate Karen's ability to engage in complex talk about her own subjective states.

Immediately after this co-narration, Karen's father retold the story, with Karen as bystander. He related what happened at Grandpa Will's house, adding background information that Karen had not included: "She threw her other one [blanket] away. Then about a week later, [she] hooked up with this one. (Unintelligible) the other day at my parents and she says, 'I don't need this anymore.' And she walked out and threw it in a garbage can . . . . I said, 'That's cool.' . . . ." As in the conversation that preceded Example 15, Karen's father took the perspective that it was time for Karen to give up her blanket. During this story, Karen was playing a board game with the researcher, and gave no sign that she was listening to her father.

Later in the taping session, Karen and her mother returned to the incident in which Karen tried to sleep without her blanket but kept dreaming about it. This co-narration was preceded by conversation in which Karen denied that she would give the researcher her blanket, "Nope, nope, nope, nope, nope, nope, nope, nope, nope, nope," and in which mother and daughter reminisced about her first special blanket, which was printed with teddy bears on one side.

Example 16: Karen (4,0) re-narrated that she dreamt about her blanket

(Beginning segment of story omitted)

Mother:	Did you miss it? I bet you did and said, "Where is my blankey (said tearfully)?"
Child:	I kept dreaming about it.
Mother:	You kept dreaming about your blankey?
Child:	Um hm.
Mother:	What were you dreaming?
Child:	I was dreaming about my blanket.
Researcher:	What happened in your dream?
Mother:	Was it a good dream, a sweet dream?
Child:	Bad dream.
Mother:	Bad, why?
Child:	Because I didn't have my blanket.

Unlike Karen's father, Karen's mother conveyed, via words and voice quality, the sadness that she imagined Karen felt—her sense of loss about the missing "blankey," an affectively charged word that harkens back to babyhood and perhaps to the teddy bear blanket that the two had discussed moments earlier.

In another long and complex story, to which Karen contributed 20 turns, she related what happened when a sick raccoon appeared on the deck of her family's house. This story is of interest for two reasons: It illustrates Karen's ability to initiate and sustain a complex narrative with minimal support except that of an interested audience, and it illustrates the salience of preference and humor as interpretive threads. In order to display Karen's narrative skill, we present the first part of the story in Karen's words, without the comments of her co-participants: "I know, there was a raccoon on our deck.... It walked, Mark (older brother) opened the door and then he shut it and he said, 'Dad, there's a raccoon on the deck.' He said that....Yeah, we, my dad kept fiddling with this thing. I can get it over there (goes to the closet to get a wooden yard stick). He kept hitting the raccoon with this (points to yard stick)..... My dad kept hitting him with that and he didn't go away but he's dead now..."

In the next section, Karen, injected humor into the story, "He's in the garbage can." In response to laughter from her audience, Karen said, "My dad said he's in raccoon heaven," to which the researcher replied, "I guess so." Karen then sarcastically disputed her father's description, "Raccoon heaven. It...'s [draws out the word] GARbage heaven," again evoking laughter, "That's cause he's in the garbage."

A few turns later, Karen asked, "Well, how can he just pick, how can he just pick our deck?" Her mother replied, "I don't know but he liked our deck," leading Karen to speculate, "Maybe he, maybe he just liked us (unintelligible)." This part of the story shows that the matter of preferences had wide and ready applicability for Karen, extending even to explanation of raccoon behavior! And it points again to Karen's creative use of interpretive frames in this sophisticated narration. The story then continued further with attention to additional details witnessed by Karen and discussion of the dangers of sick raccoons.

In sum, the Longwood children's participation in co-narrated personal storytelling had advanced a great deal by 4,0. At 2,6, the children had limited ability to relate their past experiences without the structuring prompts and questions of their more competent co-narrators, but at 4,0 they were able to narrate complex stories with little or no assistance except that of an interested and appreciative audience. They could command the floor and sustain a story in the face of genuine interlocutors. However, for the purposes of this chapter, the most important changes in the children's participation had to do with their increasingly sophisticated appropriation and creative use of the interpretive framework of child affirmation. Patrick expressed curiosity about why his mother always used the "You're so wonderful" refrain; Amy regretted that her mother had not been present to witness her athletic feat; and Karen talked about her dreams and shifting feelings and pondered a raccoon's preference.

DISCUSSION

By focusing on individual children as they navigated particular stories in context, this chapter delves more deeply into the nature of the children's engagement in personal storytelling. These analyses complicate further the intricate patterning of similarities and differences in personal storytelling as practiced by the Taipei and Longwood families.

Similarities in Meaning Making

This chapter strengthens the results of Chapter IV by demonstrating in more detail how actively the children participated in whichever version of personal storytelling their families offered. At 2,6, when their narrative skills were minimal, Yoyo and Tommy oriented verbally and nonverbally to the activity at hand and followed along while their caregivers bore most of the responsibility for the narration. Although the youngsters' subtle forms of active participation might have been missed by a casual observer, they definitely were not missed by Yoyo's grandmother and Tommy's mother. These caregivers made it possible, through their sensitive support, for their very young charges to act as co-narrators (Vygotsky, 1934/1978), while also providing opportunities for their youngsters to experience stories as bystanders.

From this baseline of mutual interest in the child's past experiences, families created stable histories of personal storytelling, which continued until at least 4 years of age. During this period, the Taipei and Longwood children played an increasingly substantial role in sustaining and developing salient cultural biases, whether by listening or narrating. As their narrative skills improved, they steered the ongoing conversation to topics that fit those biases, initiated stories, contributed novel information to the joint narration of shared experiences, selected and narrated reportable nonshared experiences, created longer story lines with minimal assistance, and used specific linguistic forms, such as story openers and conjunctions to mark temporal and causal sequencing.

The contextualized analyses presented in this chapter underscore another cultural similarity in the practice of storytelling: Stories did not exist in isolation from other stories and other discursive practices (e.g., Bauman & Briggs, 1990; Dyson, 2003; Fung, 1999; Fung & Chen, 2001; Miller & Goodnow, 1995). Rather, they formed higher order sequences. Like our earlier reports, (Fung & Chen, 2001; Miller et al., 1996), the results of this chapter suggest that this was especially pronounced in Taipei where some stories were repeated again and again. Family members and children revisited stories, recontextualizing past misdeeds and precontextualizing future or hypothetical events, traversing multiple spatial and temporal worlds (Fung & Chen, 2001). Within these practices, children's engagement was highly dynamic both within and across stories. In the course of a single co-narration (Example 3), Didi had to track and respond to the perspectives of his sister, who had witnessed his fight with Kiki, and his mother and father, who had not. When Karen's father talked about her special blanket, he adopted a matter-of-fact tone, but when Karen and her mother remembered her special blanket, they invoked feelings of loss (Example 16).

As the children gained more experience of personal storytelling, their participation became more fluent and flexible. They were able to respond deftly to their co-narrators' unfolding portrayals; to align themselves now with one participant, now with another; to change their storyline in midstream; to deploy one after another evasive strategy—all in the heat of the interaction. This kind of flexibility is a form of creativity, for each contingency is in some small way unprecedented (Bauman, 2004; Bauman & Briggs, 1990).

Differences in Meaning Making: Developing a Sense of Problem

So far, the picture that emerges from this chapter is that the children participated in personal storytelling with increasing creativity and narrative sophistication. But what was it that fueled their interest and kept them so avidly engaged? In her book *Inuit Morality Play*, Jean Briggs (1998) posed a parallel question as she traced one 3-year-old child's meaning making over time. Briggs focused on "dramas," an indigenous discursive practice that Inuit used to socialize young children. During these dramas, family members directed emotionally provocative yet playful questions to the child, repeatedly drawing her attention to particular threads of meaning. Briggs argued that over time, these threads coalesced for the child into a personally relevant and emotionally charged sense of problem that "focuses first attention and then efforts to solve or cope with the problem" (p. 209). In another paper, Briggs (1992) likened these problems and their associated questions to magnets that draw "attention to any events that might provide clues to their meanings, and to appropriate ways of dealing with the problem" (Briggs, 1992, p. 44).

Although the particular practice that led Briggs to formulate these ideas is quite different from the socializing practices identified in this monograph, we suggest that the general notion is applicable here. During the preschool years, the Taipei and Longwood families repeatedly drew their children's attention to different threads of meaning; as the children responded again and again, these threads coalesced into one sense of problem for the Taipei children and another for the Longwood children. The Taipei children seemed to develop a sense of moral problem: Did I do something wrong? How will my parents (and siblings) respond to my wrongdoing? What can I say to defend myself? How can I do better in the future? These kinds of questions reflect a finely tuned alertness to rules and to the possibility of not measuring up to moral scrutiny, a tension between faith in one's ability to improve through effort and anxiety about falling short, and a reflectiveness and curiosity about the moral domain.

The Longwood children's sense of problem did not coalesce around moral issues or their own shortcomings. The narrative practices in which they were immersed carried the message that their past misdeeds did not matter very much but that their positive qualities and preferences mattered a great deal. Given this pattern, it seems likely that they would develop a positive estimation of themselves and an expectation that others would provide a steady stream of favorable commentary. We suggest that these expectations engender a sense of problem pertaining to the maintenance of a positive self-image. What did I do well? What do I like and dislike? Do my parents (and siblings) recognize and appreciate my strengths and preferences? Does that mean that I am a smart or wonderful or funny person? What can I do to ensure other peoples' approbation? Suppose someone admonishes or criticizes me? These kinds of questions reflect a curiosity about the psychological domain and a tension between confidence in one's emerging self-definition and worry about the prospect of negative feedback.

VI. DISCUSSION

Peggy J. Miller and Shumin Lin

This project was undertaken with a dual purpose. Our primary goal was to ascertain the nature of personal storytelling as a socializing medium and everyday discursive practice in two disparate cultural worlds, extending the age range and conceptual scope of our earlier studies (Miller et al., 1996, 1997). We pursued this goal via ethnographic fieldwork combined with systematic observation of stories as they arose within the family context. This approach yielded nearly 900 stories of the children's past experiences; to our knowledge this is the largest such corpus in existence. We have already presented a discussion of each set of results in the conclusion to Chapters III–V. In this chapter, we take a larger and more integrated look at our findings, highlight the most intriguing, and pose questions for future work. The final section of the chapter addresses the second goal of this project, namely to offer an innovative conceptual and methodological approach to the study of children in cultural context.1

SOCIALIZING PATHWAYS IN TAIPEI AND LONGWOOD

Once again we begin with a familiar refrain. Each of our comparative analyses revealed a complex pattern of similarities and differences in how personal storytelling was practiced. Telling stories of young children's past experiences was a routine practice in Taipei and Longwood, occurring at remarkably similar rates and continuing apace from 2,6 to 4,0. Both sets of families told stories that encompassed a wide variety of past experiences, and both recurrently narrated children's strengths and preferences. The Taipei and Longwood children had regular access to two participant roles, co-narrator and bystander/listener, and became more active and flexible meaning makers as they got older.

These similarities coexisted with differences in the cultural frameworks that the Taipei and Longwood families used to interpret children's past experiences. Differences in baseline frequencies of occurrence and microlevel analysis of stories, along with previously reported differences in parents' explicit folk theories of childrearing, established the cultural salience of a didactic framework in Taipei and a child-affirming framework in Longwood. A major contribution of this monograph is that these differences coexisted across the entire age range with another difference, namely the privileging of the bystander/listening role in Taipei and the co-narrator role in Longwood, forming alternate socializing pathways (cf. Greenfield et al., 2003; Miller & Goodnow, 1995; Shweder et al., 2006; Weisner, 2002). Moreover, interpretive frameworks and participant roles intersected in distinct ways, revealing an affinity between listening and didactic interpretations of experience in Taipei and between co-narrating and affirming interpretations in Longwood. By applying these twin analytic perspectives of interpretive frameworks and participant roles in the context of a longitudinal design, we were able to show how threads of cultural meaning converged again and again, creating remarkable continuity across the preschool years (cf. Greenfield et al., 1989; Greenfield & Childs, 1991).

The culturally significant biases that threaded continuously through personal storytelling can be linked to the macro contexts and specific moments in history in which the Taipei and Longwood families were raising their children. As described in Chapter II, the Taipei parents grew up in an era in which traditional Confucian values were promoted across the nation and in schools as the way to create a Chinese form of modernity. Thus, it is not surprising that these values seeped into their childrearing practices (Fung, 1999; Fung et al., 2004). Although the Longwood parents wanted to preserve their neighborhood and family-centered way of life, they departed from tradition in having smaller families, and they aspired to raise their children in a new way, with a focus on fostering their self-esteem (Miller et al., 2001, Mintz, 1999). In short, both sets of parents had to negotiate the old and the new in raising their young children. The Taipei parents' didactic practices seemed to be anchored in values that bridged the traditional and the modern in the midst of dramatic material change. On the other hand, the Longwood families, living in a material world that had changed very little, seemed to anchor their affirming practices in new childrearing aspirations.

Turning now to the question of how the children navigated their respective pathways over time, the Taipei children became increasingly active moral agents when co-narrating their past transgressions: they initiated more stories on moral topics, engaged in increasingly complex moral reasoning, mitigated their own misdeeds, and even challenged the moral authority of their caregivers. Yet they continued to participate as quiet bystanders, mostly without protest, when others represented them as transgressors in past events. Moreover, they often showed subtle signs of listening; by 4 years of age they were listening to almost half of the stories that they experienced as bystanders. We conclude that the socializing pathway created by the Taipei caregivers and children involved two critical elements, both of which were morally inflected: learning to become a sophisticated, autonomous moral agent and learning to listen quietly. The Taipei children's navigation of this pathway toward self-improvement may have been supported by their adjacent experience of stories in which their caregivers narrated their cognitive and moral strengths, praising them for their persistence, concentration, and patience in learning.

By contrast, the medium of personal storytelling, whether configured as co-narrations or bystander stories, afforded the Longwood children minimal opportunity for moral reasoning other than recognizing and celebrating their own goodness. Personal storytelling was simply not a venue for discussing children's past transgressions or shortcomings, raising the question of how they received negative feedback. On the rare occasion that a misdeed slipped into the narrative record, it was downplayed or laughed about. Instead, personal storytelling provided a forum in which family members accepted children's preferences and accentuated their strengths, with the latter becoming more frequent over time. This child-affirming interpretive framework coexisted with the privileging of the co-narrator role, creating a socializing pathway in which children became more active in voicing their strengths and preferences and honing their sense of humor. Child affirmation and child self-expression converged in these narrative practices.

Taken together, our findings extend our earlier work by establishing that personal storytelling was part and parcel of young children's everyday family life throughout the entire age range. They support LeVine and Norman's (2001) claim that parents begin very early in the child's life to cultivate local models of virtue. Our work adds a new twist to this argument by showing that parents may use narrative to deliver such "head starts." And it helps to explain how children might develop a precocious grasp of local models of virtue: socialization not only begins very early but it is also intense, continuous, and prolonged. The families in our study invested an enormous amount of time and energy in these narrative practices. No wonder that the Taipei children emerged as precocious in the realms of listening and moral reasoning, the Longwood children in self-affirmation and self-expression. The continuity that we discovered in the preschool years raises the question of what happens later in the children's lives and whether this continuity will extend into maturity. When they become parents, will their narrative practices carry echoes of the salient cultural biases that they experienced as children?

Our findings also underscore the intricacy of personal storytelling as a differentiated medium of socialization and suggest that multiple levels of analysis need to be taken into account to fully appreciate this complexity. These levels of analysis include content, structure, and function of stories; modes of participation; and higher order sequencing of stories in relation to other stories and other discursive practices. Within each cultural case, particular threads of meaning were discernible across levels of analysis. It is the interweaving of these threads—some similar, some subtly different, some radically different—that yielded the distinct texture and color of socializing pathways in Taipei and Longwood.

In sum, our findings do not support a dichotomous or monolithic reading of cultural differences (Ochs, 1999). We use the terms "threads of meaning," "versions of personal storytelling," "alternative lenses," and "cultural biases or slants on experience" to emphasize this point. As discussed in Chapter III, although the didactic lens took precedence for the Taipei families, their assiduous pedagogical attention to children's misdeeds did not prevent them from narrating their children's strengths and recognizing their preferences. Also, it is important to remember that many stories told by the Longwood and Taipei families did not carry the salient interpretive frameworks that we have focused on in this monograph. A full account of the socializing potential of personal storytelling in each community would have to go beyond the didactic and affirming to examine other cultural biases embodied in personal storytelling (e.g., different ways of interpreting social bonds). On the other hand, it is also important to remember that the cultural salience of the didactic and affirming practices was also apparent in other discursive practices in these families (Fung, 1999; Haight et al., 1999).

THE POWER OF RECURRENCE AND REPETITION

We argue that the cultural slants identified in this report leave a powerful mark on participants and that they do so, in part, through their sheer frequency. Because the children encountered so many stories in their everyday lives, these slants were unavoidable. Particular frameworks of interpretation, evaluation, and participation, linked to larger currents of cultural meaning, operated again and again, whether in stories of different past experiences or in repetitions of the "same" story. As argued by Fung and Chen (2001) and established in Chapter V, family members and young children traversed multiple temporal and spatial worlds as they navigated within stories and across sequences of stories and other discursive practices. Each encounter required that narrators and listeners create and respond to here-and-now social contingencies. Thus, a major contribution of this monograph is that it opens a window on how socialization operates on the ground: socialization through personal storytelling is a highly dynamic process in which redundancy and variation are conjoined (Fung & Chen, 2001; Miller et al., 1996). Children's participation, even at 2,6, was not fixed or mechanical but flexible.

The recurring and repetitive nature of personal storytelling also helps to explain how personal storytelling operates holistically in children's lives and infiltrates their hearts and minds. Each didactic or affirming story provided another opportunity for the child to hear which of her experiences were reportable, how her actions were related, and how her experiences should be assessed. In this way cultural slants on experience were not only reproduced but also repeatedly instantiated in personally relevant terms. It was the child himself who violated a rule or behaved kindly. And it was the child's parent who interpreted his behavior in this way or that. In other words, the repeated instantiation of cultural slants was doubling personalizing, for they were applied *to* the child's personal experience *by* the most important persons in the child's life. In short, children's engagement in storytelling could not be neutral or distant because so much was at stake; this affectively charged interpretive practice was the matrix within which their senses of problem took shape (Briggs, 1998). Here we also see how culturally tinged selves might originate. A need for positive self-regard (Heine, Lehman, Markus, & Kitayama, 1999) may be rooted, in part, in storytelling that is systematically biased in a child-affirming direction, whereas an inclination to self-improvement (Li, 2004a) may be rooted, in part, in the narration of misdeeds and the expectation of improvement.

This understanding of socialization accords well with Quinn's (2005b) synthesis of anthropological work on childrearing. Quinn argues that although cultural models of childrearing are highly variable in the substance of what is taught, all are designed to "make the child's experience of those lessons constant, to link those lessons to emotional arousal, to connect them to evaluations of the child, as approved or disapproved of, and to prime the child to be emotionally predisposed to learn them. This design insures that the child is receptive to these lessons, and that the lessons themselves are unmistakable, motivating, and memorable." (p. 477). Perhaps, one reason why disparate cultures have used personal storytelling to socialize children is that it is such an effective way to convey such lessons.

We also affirm Quinn's (2005b) point that these lessons are especially powerfully communicated by means of implicit messages, such as those conveyed by body language (e.g., Yoyo's grandmother held him in her arms while reviewing his misdeeds and laughed when he said, "give me a tender touch"), by selecting some events (e.g., Karen's attachment to her blanket) to revisit again and again, by casting the child more often as co-narrator or more often as bystander. Quinn singles out, in particular, the messages implicit in that which the child does *not* experience: her misdeeds are not revisited and her preferences and dispreferences are not disapproved of; alternatively, her strengths are not inflated and her misdeeds are not overlooked.

An important implication of this feature of socialization is that parents will be only partially aware of the nature of their own practices. In interviews, mothers in Taipei and Longwood placed a high value on personal narrative as a family practice and gave many examples of adults telling stories (Miller et al., 2001). Interestingly, however, they showed little if any awareness of the narrative practices that are the focus of this monograph, namely those involving young children as protagonists and participants (Miller et al., 2001). This finding is reminiscent of Briggs's (1998) finding that Inuit adults routinely orchestrated "dramas" with young children, but these dramas were never mentioned by Inuit adults when they talked about childrearing. The fact that caregivers in these various cases engaged routinely in socializing practices of which they had little awareness underscores another important implication of recurrence and repetition, namely that such practices can become increasingly habitualized and taken-for-granted over time (Bourdieu, 1990; Miller & Goodnow, 1995).

But mothers in our study did talk explicitly about some of their childrearing goals, including opportunity education in Taipei and fostering children's self-esteem in Longwood (Fung, 1999; Miller et al., 2001; Mintz, 1999). Although no parent in either cultural case advocated *using personal stories* to teach moral values (Taipei) or foster their child's self-esteem (Longwood), they routinely enacted interpretive frameworks compatible with these respective childrearing goals. This intriguing discrepancy in which adults were able to do more than they could say has long been recognized in scholarship on practice approaches to language (e.g., Hanks, 1996; Hymes, 1975; Silverstein, 1981), but it is rarely recognized in research on socialization and could not have been discovered here without documenting parents' participation in routine practices. A more commonly recognized discrepancy in developmental research on socialization is that parents' observed practices may fall short of their self-reported goals. Thus, another contribution of this monograph is to complicate the problem of consciousness/unconsciousness, raising the following question for future research: which aspects of parents' socializing goals and practices are parents aware of, under what conditions, and to what degree?

There is one final point to be made on the issue of parents' tacit understandings of socializing practices. Both groups of parents in this study seemed to operate on the tacit assumption that personal storytelling is a potent socializing tool. This tacit premise slots easily into the Taipei parents' didacticism; given parents' responsibility to teach their children, it makes sense to use stories of past misdeeds to deliver and reinforce socializing messages. But what about the Longwood parents? Their inclination to keep negative images out of stories while loading stories with affirming images of the child may rest on a similar assumption but with a different rationale: because negative feedback is potentially damaging to children's psychological well-being and self-esteem and because stories are powerful interpretive tools, parents should not dwell on children's past misdeeds. Rather, they should correct children's misdeeds when they happen, thereby bypassing the potential of stories to reinforce unwanted negative messages (see Miller et al., 1997). If this speculation is correct, disciplinary practices in the here-and-now would be the place to look to determine how Longwood parents and their children handle negative feedback.

REVALUING LISTENING AND CO-NARRATING

Another intriguing finding of this monograph is that the Taipei children, compared with their Longwood counterparts, engaged in much more listening from the vantage point of the bystander role, an advantage that they retained across the age span. This kind of listening dovetailed with the didactic slant of the Taipei families' interpretive framework and with other studies that point to a concern with moral correctness in the socialization of children in various Chinese groups (Chao, 1994; Wang & Leichtman, 2000; Wang et al., 2000; Wang et al., 2008). Our findings add weight to Jin Li's (2003a, 2003b, 2004a) argument that Chinese models of learning, inflected in a Confucian direction, envision learning as a moral project in the service of self-perfection. These models imply that listening is not a neutral matter of imbibing information but a moral act involving respect and affection for caregivers, as moral authorities. By contrast, the privileging of the co-narrator role in Longwood, together with the expression of children's strengths, preferences, and humor, color the parent-child role relationship rather differently. Parents are not so much moral authorities, whose higher status and greater life experience require respect. Rather, they are collaborators with young children, guardians of their well-being, and audience to their exploits, supporting their involvement in the project of self-enhancement and expression of an inner self (Cho et al., 2005; Miller et al., 2002).

Another implication of our findings on listening is that the Taipei children had the benefit of more overall narrative experience. Even though their past experiences were narrated at rates and lengths that were roughly equivalent to their Longwood counterparts', the Taipei children paid attention to a considerably larger subset of bystander stories. They kept their ears "open" most of the time and thus could learn about storytelling through both silent listening and co-narrating. The Longwood children, on the other hand, listened to few bystander stories, and this disadvantage was not entirely offset by their higher rate of participation in co-narrations. This may help to explain why the Longwood children did not incur more of a developmental advantage as co-narrators at the later ages. In short, we believe that our results underscore the need for further exploration of listening as a mode of learning in and from storytelling. Future work will have to grapple with the methodological problem of how to study listening more precisely. It will also need to tease apart what children learn from *listening in* (listening as a bystander), as against what they learn from listening as an inherent part of co-narrating.

Our findings also contribute fresh evidence that listening/observing is a universal mode of learning, which nonetheless varies widely across cultures in its degree of cultural elaboration (Gaskins & Paradise, 2010). The best examples of listening as a highly valued and pervasive mode of learning have come from small-scale traditional societies (Childs & Greenfield, 1980; Gaskins & Paradise, 2010; Greenfield, 1984; Rogoff et al., 2003, 2007). The Taiwanese families—middle-class, educated, urban, members of a large-scale "modern" society—add a very different case to the mix of culturally elaborated versions of listening. Yet the Taipei children, like their Mayan counterparts, were creative listeners who go far beyond mimicking what they see and hear (Rogoff et al., 2003). On the other hand, our findings do not support a linear trajectory from legitimate peripheral participation to central participation (Lave & Wenger, 1991; Rogoff et al., 2003, 2007). Listening from the vantage point of the bystander role did not wane as the Taipei children advanced as co-narrators. And even in Longwood, where the bystander role occurred far less frequently, children continued to listen in about one-fifth of the bystander stories at 4,0. These findings suggest that the bystander/listener and the co-narrator roles were coexisting routes by which children learned to participate in storytelling.

Moreover, we submit that these analytically distinct routes comingled in the children's experience (Miller, Hengst, Alexander, & Sperry, 2000; Sperry & Sperry, 2000). The personal stories in which they participated were not compartmentalized as co-narrated stories, on the one hand, and bystander stories on the other. This means that what a child learned from co-narrations could inform her participation in bystander stories and vice versa. For example, although Taipei parents infrequently urged their children to listen—perhaps because the children already displayed listening from an early age—such explicit exhortations occurred only during co-narrations. Example 3 in Chapter III illustrates this well: unnerved by the memory of Didi getting lost at the night market, his mother constructed a lengthy coda in which she implored him to listen to her and his father so that he would not endanger himself in the future. Such affectively charged pleas are likely to be remembered by children and may encourage them to adopt a general stance of keeping their ears open.

There is one final point about our findings on children's participant roles. Fung et al. (2003) argued that many developmental studies of narrative, shaped by North American cultural assumptions, have implicitly privileged the (co) narrator role over the listener role, treating listening as passive and uninteresting. The findings of Chapter IV compelled us to reflect further on hidden cultural assumptions about listening and to realize that the term "co-narrator" harbors such assumptions. In fact, children cannot participate in co-narrations without listening to their coparticipants' contributions, yet this term names one part of the process and elides the other; a more accurate term would be "co-narrator/co-listener." In short, our findings on children's participation highlights the need for a more balanced approach that examines the socializing value of both listening and narrating, with openness to the diverse forms that each might take.

OUR METHODOLOGICAL APPROACH

Apart from its substantive goals, the research presented here was undertaken with the aim of contributing to the evolving conversation about how to recoup a deeper and more nuanced understanding of development and culture as intertwined processes (e.g., Briggs, 1998; Garcia Coll & Marks, 2009; Gaskins et al., 1992; Jessor et al., 1996; Rogoff et al., 1993; Shweder et al., 2006; Weisner, 2005). We combined ethnographic fieldwork and interviews with longitudinal home observations and microlevel analysis of stories in context, a mode of inquiry derived from interdisciplinary research on discursive practices. Our strongest argument in support of this approach consists in the foregoing findings and the questions for future work that they engendered. We sought to understand the process of everyday socialization as embedded in local ecologies and historically and culturally situated systems of meaning. Given this problem, we argue that there is no substitute for tracking discursive practices when, where, and as they happen (Miller et al., 2011). By documenting the routine narrative practices that families used in their homes, it was possible to show just how dynamic the socializing process was and to follow in the interpretive footsteps of individual children as they navigated stories over time. It was also possible to see how storytelling was embedded in the flow of social interaction, forming higher order sequences of narratives and other discursive practices. More conventional methods for studying socialization (e.g., questionnaire measures of parents' childrearing beliefs and child outcomes or observations of preselected tasks) yield important insights into socialization, but they cannot address the problem that lies at the heart of this monograph.

Another methodological feature that deserves mention is the time-honored ethnographic strategy of comparing particular cases, each of which is described in great contextualized detail (Erickson, 1986; Gaskins et al., 1992; Miller et al., 2003). Like the parents in this study, ethnographers harbor many taken-for-granted assumptions rooted in their own cultural experience. We believe that it would have been much harder to "see" certain patterns in the Taipei and Longwood stories without having to commute back and forth between the two. Cultural omissions (e.g., not narrating misdeeds) are notoriously hard to spot without a vantage point outside one's own culture.

However, like any method, our approach has limitations. A significant practical limitation is the labor-intensive nature of ethnographic fieldwork, longitudinal observation, transcription, and microlevel analysis of talk. From the standpoint of most research in developmental psychology, a more serious limitation is the small sample size, raising questions about the generalizability of our findings. Much ethnographic research does not seek to generalize beyond the cultural case at hand but rather to determine how a particular case, described in great contextualized detail, compares to the universe of other such cases (Erickson, 1986). Although no other study has used our approach to compare narrative socialization in Taiwan and the United States, throughout this monograph, we have discussed our findings alongside relevant developmental research on socialization in Taiwan (and other Chinese communities) and North America. Importantly, the cultural slants that we identified converged with other findings from studies using other methods (e.g., Chao, 1994; Fung et al., 2003; Li, 2002; Wang & Leichtman, 2000; Wang et al., 2000; Wang et al., 2008). This suggests the viability of mixed-methods designs, combining in-depth contextualized analyses of discursive practices in a small number of participants with more conventional studies involving larger sample sizes.

Our methods can also be criticized for not being fine-grained enough. Some language socialization researchers use conversation analytic methods, which are more precise than the level of description adopted here (e.g., Ochs & Capps, 2001; Taylor, 1995). Conversation analysis is based on line-by-line description of segments of naturally-occurring talk, including interruptions, overlaps, stress, voice quality, and measurement of pauses between speakers' turns at talk. This kind of analysis captures the complexity of talk in more detail than we have done, but it is even more time-consuming, precluding analysis of a corpus of stories as large as ours. Thus, we made a methodological choice to balance precision and scope.

In conclusion, the overarching contribution of this monograph is to provide deeper insight into childhood socialization as a contextualized process of breathtaking intricacy and dynamism. This contribution could not have been achieved without an innovative combination of ethnography and close analysis of everyday discursive practices over time. These methods allowed us to expose the subtle patterning of cultural similarities and differences in personal storytelling, as practiced in Taipei and Longwood, without subduing the complexity of distinct meaning in each. In this way, to paraphrase Jean Briggs (1992), we glimpse something of the shapes, always changing, always incomplete, of the worlds that the Taipei and Longwood children were building, and, more important, we see the building process itself (p. 45).

REFERENCES

Au, K. H. (1993). *Literacy instruction in multicultural settings.* Fort Worth, TX: Harcourt Brace Jovanovich College Publishers.

Bamberg, M. (1997). *Narrative development.* Mahwah, NJ: Erlbaum.

Basso, K. (1996). *Wisdom sits in places: Landscape and language among the Western Apache.* Albuquerque, NM: University of New Mexico Press.

Bauman, R. (2004). *A world of others' words: Cross-cultural perspectives on intertextuality.* Malden, MA: Blackwell Publishing.

Bauman, R., & Briggs, C. L. (1990). Poetics and performance as critical perspectives on language and social life. *Annual Review of Anthropology,* **19,** 59–88.

Becker, H. S. (1996). The epistemology of qualitative research. In R. Jessor, A. Colby, & R. Shweder (Eds.), *Ethnography and human development: Context and meaning in social inquiry* (pp. 53–72). Chicago: University of Chicago Press.

Bloom, L. (1974). Commentary. In F. F. Schachter, K. Kirshner, B. Klips, M. Friedricks, & K. Sanders (Eds.), *Everyday preschool interpersonal speech usage: Methodological, development, and sociolinguistic studies. Monographs of the Society for Research in Child Development,* **39**(3, Serial No. 156, pp. 82–88).

Bourdieu, P. (1990). *The logic of practice.* Stanford, CA: Stanford University Press.

Brady, M. K. (1984). *Some kind of power: Navajo children's skinwalker narratives.* Salt Lake City: Utah University Press.

Briggs, C. (1986). *Learning how to ask.* New York: Cambridge University Press.

Briggs, J. L. (1970). *Never in anger: Portrait of an Eskimo family.* Cambridge, MA: Harvard University Press.

Briggs, J. L. (1992). Mazes of meaning: How a child and a culture create each other. In W. A. Corsaro & P. J. Miller (Eds.), *Interpretive approaches to children's socialization. New directions for child and adolescent development* (Issue No. 58, pp. 25–49). San Francisco: Jossey-Bass.

Briggs, J. L. (1998). *Inuit morality play: The emotional education of a three-year-old.* New Haven, CT: Yale University Press.

Bruner, J. S. (1990). *Acts of meaning.* Cambridge, MA: Harvard University Press.

Byatt, A. S. (2001). *On histories and stories: Selected essays.* Cambridge, MA: Harvard University Press.

Chao, R. (1994). Beyond parental control & authoritarian parenting style: Understanding Chinese parenting through the cultural notion of training. *Child Development,* **65,** 1111–1119.

Chase, S. (2008). *Perfectly prep: Gender extremes at a New England prep school.* New York: Oxford University Press.

Chen, X., Hastings, P., Rubin, K. H., Chen, H., Cen, G., & Stewart, S. L. (1998). Childrearing attitudes and behavioral inhibition in Chinese and Canadian toddlers: A cross-cultural study. *Developmental Psychology*, **34**, 677–686.

Chen, X., Rubin, K. H., & Li, Z. (1995). Social functioning and adjustment in Chinese children: A longitudinal study. *Developmental Psychology*, **31**, 531–539.

Childs, C. P., & Greenfield, P. M. (1980). Informal modes of learning and teaching: The case of Zinacanteco weaving. In N. Warren, (Ed.), *Studies in cross-cultural psychology*, (Vol. **2**, pp. 269–316). London: Academic Press.

Cho, G. E., & Miller, P. J. (2004). Personal storytelling: Working-class and middle-class mothers in comparative perspective. In M. Farr (Ed.), *Ethnolinguistic Chicago: Language and literacy in Chicago's neighborhoods* (pp. 79–101). Mahwah, NJ: Erlbaum.

Cho, G. E., Miller, P. J., Sandel, T., & Wang, S.-H. (2005). What do grandmothers think about self-esteem? American and Taiwanese folk theories revisited. *Social Development*, **14**, 701–721.

Chu, C. L. (1972). Cong shehui geren yu wenhua de guanxi lun zhongguo ren de chigan quxiang [On the shame orientation of the Chinese from the interrelationship among society, individual, and culture]. In I. Y. Lee & K. S. Yang (Eds.), *Zhongguo ren de xingge: Keji zonghe xing de taolun [Symposium on the character of the Chinese: An interdisciplinary approach]* (pp. 85–125). Taipei, Taiwan: Institute of Ethnology, Academia Sinica.

Clark, C. D. (2003). *In sickness and in play: Children coping with chronic illness*. New Brunswick, NJ: Rutgers University Press.

Cohen, M. J. (1988). *Taiwan at the crossroads*. Washington, DC: Asia Resource Center.

Cole, M. (1996). *Cultural psychology: A once and future discipline*. Cambridge, MA: Harvard University Press.

Corsaro, W. A. (1985). *Friendship and peer culture in the early years*. Norwood, NJ: Ablex.

Corsaro, W. A. (2003). *"We're friends, right?": Inside kids' culture*. Washington, DC: Joseph Henry Press.

Corsaro, W. A. (2005). *The sociology of childhood*. Thousand Oaks, CA: Pine Forge Press.

Corsaro, W. A., & Miller, P. J. (Eds.). (1992). Interpretive approaches to children's socialization. *New directions for child and adolescent development* (Issue No. 58). San Francisco: Jossey-Bass.

Corsaro, W. A., & Molinari L., & Rosier, K. B. (2002). Zena and Carlotta: Transition narratives and early education in the United States and Italy. *Human Development*, **45**, 323–348.

Daiute, C., & Lightfoot, C. (Eds.). (2004). *Narrative analysis: Studying the development of individuals in society*. Thousand Oaks, CA: Sage.

Damon, W., & Lerner, R. M. (Eds.). (2006). *Handbook of child psychology* (6th ed.). Hoboken, NJ: John Wiley & Sons.

Denzin, N. K., & Lincoln, Y. (Eds.). (2005). *Handbook of qualitative research* (3rd ed.). Thousands Oaks, CA: Sage Publications.

Duncan, G. J., Huston, A. C., & Weisner, T. S. (2007). *Higher ground: New hope for the working poor and their children*. New York: Russell Sage.

Duneier, M. (1999). *Sidewalk*. New York: Farrar Strauss.

Duranti, A., & Goodwin, C. (Eds.). (1992). *Rethinking context: Language as an interactive phenomenon*. New York: Cambridge University Press.

Duranti, A., Ochs, E., & Schieffelin, B. B. (Eds.). (2011). *Handbook of language socialization*. Malden, MA: Wiley-Blackwell.

Dyson, A. H. (2003). *The brothers and sisters learn to write: Popular literacies in childhood and school cultures*. New York: Teachers College Press.

Dyson, A. H., & Genishi, C. (Eds.). (1994). *The need for story: Cultural diversity in classroom and community*. Urbana, IL: National Council of Teachers of English.

Emde, R. N., Wolf, D. P., & Oppenheim, D. (Eds.). (2003). *Revealing the inner worlds of young children.* New York: Oxford University Press.

Emerson, R. M., Fretz, R., & Shaw, L. L. (1995). *Writing ethnographic fieldnotes.* Chicago: University of Chicago Press.

Engel, S. (1995). *The stories children tell: Making sense of the narrative of childhood.* New York: W. H. Freeman.

Erickson, F. (1986). Qualitative methods in research on teaching. In M. C. Wittrock (Ed.), *Handbook of research on teaching* (3rd ed., pp. 119–161). New York: Macmillan.

Farris, C. S. P. (1988). *Language and sex role acquisition in a Taiwanese kindergarten: A semiotic analysis.* Unpublished doctoral dissertation, University of Washington, Seattle.

Fiese, B. H. (2006). *Family routines and rituals.* New Haven, CT: Yale University Press.

Fivush, R., & Haden, C. (Eds.). (2003). *Autobiographical memory and the construction of a narrative self: Developmental and cultural perspectives.* Hillsdale, NJ: Erlbaum.

Fivush, R., & Hammond, N. R. (1990). Autobiographical memory across the preschool years: Toward reconceptualizing childhood amnesia. In R. Fivish & J. Hudson (Eds.), *Knowing and remembering in young children* (pp. 223–248). New York: Cambridge University Press.

Fivush, R., & Nelson, K. (2006). Parent-child reminiscing locates the self in the past. *British Journal of Developmental Psychology, 24,* 235–251.

Fivush, R., & Wang, Q. (2005). Emotion talk in mother-child conversations of the shared past: The effects of culture, gender, and event valence. *Journal of Cognition and Development, 6,* 489–506.

Fung, H. (1994). *The socialization of shame in young Chinese children.* Unpublished doctoral dissertation, University of Chicago.

Fung, H. (1999). Becoming a moral child: The socialization of shame among young Chinese children. *Ethos, 27,* 180–209.

Fung, H. (2006). Affect and early moral socialization: Some insights and contributions from indigenous psychological studies in Taiwan. In U. Kim, K. S. Yang, & K. K. Hwang (Eds.), *Indigenous and cultural psychology: Understanding people in context* (pp. 175–196). New York: Springer.

Fung, H., & Chen, E. C.-H. (2001). Across time and beyond skin: Self and transgression in the everyday socialization of shame among Taiwanese preschool children [Special issue on social interaction: The dual development of communication and social relationships]. *Social Development, 10,* 419–436.

Fung, H., Lieber, E., & Leung, P. W. L. (2003). Parental beliefs on shame and moral socialization in Taiwan, Hong Kong, and the United States. In K. S. Yang, K. K. Hwang, P. B. Pedersen, & I. Daibo (Eds.), *Progress in Asian social psychology: Conceptual and empirical contributions* (pp. 83–109). Westport, CT: Praeger Publishers.

Fung, H., Miller, P. J., & Lin, L.-C. (2004). Listening is active: Lessons from the narrative practices of Taiwanese families. In M. W. Pratt & B. E. Fiese (Eds.), *Family stories and the life course: Across time and generations* (pp. 303–323). Mahwah, NJ: Erlbaum.

Gao, G. (1998). "Don't take my word for it"—Understanding Chinese speaking practices. *International Journal of Intercultural Relations, 22,* 163–186.

Garcia Coll, C., & Marks, A. K. (2009). *Immigrant stories: Ethnicity and academics in middle childhood.* New York: Oxford University Press.

Garrett, P. B., & Baquedano-López, P. (2002). Language socialization: Reproduction and continuity, transformation and change. *Annual Review of Anthropology, 31,* 339–361.

Gaskins, S. (1996). How Mayan parental theories come into play. In S. Harkness & M. Super (Eds.), *Parents' cultural belief systems: Their origins, expressions, and consequences* (pp. 345–363). New York: Guilford.

Gaskins, S. (1999). Children's daily lives in a Mayan village: A case study of culturally constructed roles and activities. In A. Göncü (Ed.), *Children's engagement in the world* (pp. 25–81). Cambridge, UK: Cambridge University Press.

Gaskins, S., Miller, P. J., & Corsaro, W. A. (1992). Theoretical and methodological perspectives in the interpretive study of children. In W.A. Corsaro & P. J. Miller (Eds.), *Interpretive approaches to children's socialization* (pp. 5–23). San Francisco: Jossey-Bass.

Gaskins, S. & Paradise, R. (2010). Learning through observation. In D. F. Lancy, J. Brock, & S. Gaskins, (Eds.), (*The anthropology of learning in childhood* (pp. 85–117). Lanham, MD: Alta Mira Press.

Goffman, E. (1979). Footing. *Semiotica,* **25**, 1–29.

Gold, T. B. (1986). *State and society in the Taiwan miracle.* Armonk, NY: M. E. Sharpe.

Göncü, A. (Ed.). (1999). *Children's engagement in the world: Sociocultural perspectives.* Cambridge, UK: Cambridge University Press.

Goodnow, J. J., Miller, P. J., & Kessel, F. (Eds.). (1995). Cultural practices as contexts for development. *New directions for child and adolescent development* (Issue No. 67). San Francisco: Jossey-Bass.

Gottlieb, A. (2004). *The afterlife is where we came from: The culture of infancy in West Africa.* Chicago: University of Chicago Press.

Greenfield, P. M. (1984). A theory of the teacher in the learning activities of everyday life. In B. Rogoff & J. Lave (Eds.), *Everyday cognition* (pp. 117–138). Cambridge, MA: Harvard University Press.

Greenfield, P. M., Brazelton, T. B., & Childs, C. P. (1989). From birth to maturity in Zinacantan: Ontogenesis in cultural context. In V. Bricker & G. Gossen (Eds.), *Ethnographic encounters in Southern Mesoamerica: Celebratory essays in honor of Evon Z. Vogt* (pp. 177–216). Albany: Institute of Mesoamerican Studies, State University of New York.

Greenfield, P. M., & Childs, C. P. (1991). Developmental continuity in biocultural context. In R. Cohen & A. W. Siegel (Eds.), *Context and development* (pp. 135–159). Hillsdale, NJ: Lawrence Erlbaum.

Greenfield, P. M., Keller, H., Fuligni, A., & Maynard, A. (2003). Cultural pathways through universal development. *Annual Review of Psychology,* **54**, 461–490.

Greenfield, P. M., Suzuki, L. K., & Rothstein-Fisch, C. (2006). Culture pathways through human development. In W. Damon, R. M. Lerner (Series Eds.), K. A. Renninger, & I. E. Sigel (Vol. Eds.), *Handbook of child psychology: Vol. 4. Child psychology in practice* (6th ed., pp. 655–699). New York: Wiley.

Haden, C. A., Haine, R. A., & Fivush, R. (1997). Developing narrative structure in parent-child reminiscing across the preschool years. *Developmental Psychology,* **33**, 295–307.

Haight, W. L., Wang, X.-L., Fung, H., Williams, K., & Mintz, J. (1999) Universal, developmental, and variable aspects of young children's play: A cross-cultural comparison of pretending at home. *Child Development,* **70**, 1477–1488.

Hammersley, M., & Atkinson, P. (1995). *Ethnography: Principles in practice* (2nd ed.). New York: Routledge.

Hanks, W. (1996). *Language and communicative practice.* Boulder, CO: Westview Press.

Harkness, S., & Super, C. M. (1977). Why African children are so hard to test. In L. L. Adler (Ed.), *Issues in cross-cultural research* (pp. 326–337). New York: The New York Academy of Sciences.

Harkness, S., & Super, M. (Eds.) (1996). *Parents' cultural belief systems: Their origins, expressions, and consequences.* New York: Guilford.

Harwood, R. L., Miller, J. G., & Irizarry, N. L. (1995). *Culture and attachment: Perceptions of the child in context.* New York: Guilford Press.

Harwood, R. L., Schoelmerich, A., Schulze, P. A., & Gonzalez, Z. (1999). Cultural differences in maternal beliefs and behaviors: A study of middle-class Anglo and Puerto Rican mother-infant pairs in four everyday situations. *Child Development*, **70**, 1005–1016.

He, A. W. (2001). The language of ambiguity: Practices in Chinese heritage language classes. *Discourse Studies*, **3**, 75–96.

Heath, S. B. (1983). *Ways with words: Language, life, and work in communities and classrooms.* New York: Cambridge University Press.

Heine, S. H., Lehman, D. R., Markus, H. R., & Kitayama, S. (1999). Is there a universal need for positive self-regard? *Psychological Review*, **106**, 766–794.

Ho, D. Y. F. (1986). Chinese patterns of socialization: A critical review. In M. H. Bond (Ed.), *The handbook of Chinese psychology* (pp. 155–165). Hong Kong: Oxford University Press.

Holland, D., Lachicotte, W., Skinner, D., & Cain C. (1998). *Identity and agency in cultural worlds.* Cambridge, MA: Harvard University Press.

Hsiao, H. H. M. (Ed.). (1989). *Bianqian zhong taiwan shehui di zhongchan jieji. [The middle class in the changing Taiwan society].* Taipei, Taiwan: Chui-Lui Press.

Hsu, F. L. K. (1971). *Under the ancestors' shadow: Kinship, personality, and social mobility in China.* Stanford, CA: University Press.

Hsu, F. L. K. (1983). *Rugged individualism reconsidered: Essays in psychology anthropology.* Knoxville: University of Tennessee Press.

Hudley, E. P., Haight, W. L., & Miller, P. J. (2003). *"Raise up a child": Human development in an African-American family.* Chicago: Lyceum.

Hymes, D. (1975). Breakthrough into performance. In D. Ben-Amos & K. S. Goldenstein (Eds.), *Folklore: Performance and communication* (pp. 11–74). The Hague, The Netherlands: Mouton.

Hymes, D. (1996). *Ethnography, linguistics, narrative inequality: Toward an understanding of voice.* London: Taylor & Francis.

Jessor, R., Colby, A., & Shweder, R. (Eds.). (1996). *Ethnography and human development: Context and meaning in social inquiry.* Chicago: University of Chicago Press.

Kerr, G, II. (1965). *Formosa betrayed.* Boston: Houghton Mifflin Co.

Kim, H. S. (2002). We talk, therefore we think? A cultural analysis of the effect of talking on thinking. *Journal of Personality and Social Psychology*, **83**, 828–842.

Kim, H. S., & Markus, H. R. (2002). Freedom of speech and freedom of silence: An analysis of talking as a cultural practice. In R. Shweder, M. Minow, & H. R. Markus (Eds.), *Engaging cultural differences: The multicultural challenge in liberal democracies* (pp. 432–452). New York: Russell Sage Foundation.

Koven, M. (2007). *Selves in two languages: Bilingual verbal enactments of identity in French and Portuguese.* Amsterdam: John Benjamins.

Kulick, D., & Schieffelin, B. (2004). Language socialization. In A. Duranti (Ed.), *A companion to linguistic anthropology* (pp. 349–368). Oxford, UK: Blackwell.

Larson, R., & Jensen, L. (Eds.). (2005). *New horizons, new directions for child development.* San-Francisco: Jossey-Bass.

Lave, J., & Wenger, E. (1991). *Situated learning: Legitimate peripheral participation.* New York: Cambridge University Press.

Leeds-Hurwitz, W. (2005). Ethnography. In K. L. Fitch & R. E. Sanders (Eds.), *Handbook of language and social interaction* (pp. 327–353). Mahwah, NJ: Erlbaum.

LeVine, R. A., LeVine, S., Dixon, S., Richman, A., Leiderman, P. H., Keefer, C. H., et al. (1994). *Child care and culture: Lessons from Africa.* New York: Cambridge University Press.

LeVine, R. A., & Norman, K. (2001). The infant's acquisition of culture: Early attachment reexamined in anthropological perspective. In C. C. Moore & H. F. Matthews (Eds.), *The psychology of cultural experience* (pp. 83–104). New York: Cambridge University Press.

Li, J. (2002). A cultural model of learning: Chinese "heart and mind for wanting to learn." *Journal of Cross-Cultural Psychology, 33*, 248–269.

Li, J. (2003a). U.S. and Chinese cultural beliefs about learning. *Journal of Educational Psychology, 95*, 258–267.

Li, J. (2003b). The core of Confucian learning. *American Psychologist, 58*, 146–147.

Li, J. (2004a). Learning as a task or a virtue: U.S. and Chinese preschoolers explain learning. *Developmental Psychology, 40*, 595–605.

Li, J. (2004b). "I learn and I grow big": Chinese preschoolers' purposes for learning. *International Journal of Behavioral Development, 28*, 116–128.

Li, J. (2009). *To speak or not to speak: Context sensitivity in speaking among Chinese.* Unpublished data, Brown University, Providence, RI.

Lieber, E., Fung, H., & Leung, P. W. L. (2006). Chinese child-rearing beliefs: Key dimensions and the development of culture-appropriate assessment. *Asian Journal of Social Psychology, 9*, 140–147.

Lin, S. (2009). How listening is silenced: A monolingual Taiwanese elder constructs identity through television viewing. *Language in Society, 38*, 311–337.

Lutz, C., & White, G. M. (1986). The anthropology of emotion. *Annual Review of Anthropology, 15*, 405–436.

MacWhinney, B. (1991). *The CHILDES project: Tools for analyzing talk.* Hillsdale, NJ: Erlbaum.

Malinowski, B. (1922). *Argonauts of the Western Pacific.* London: Routledge & Kegan Paul.

Mandelbaum, D. G. (Ed.). (1951). *Selected writings of Edward Sapir in language, culture, and personality.* Berkeley: University of California Press.

Markus, H. R., & Kitayama, S. (1994). The cultural construction of self and emotion: Implications for social behavior. In S. Kitayama & H. R. Markus (Eds.), *Emotion and culture: Empirical studies of mutual influences* (pp. 89–130). Washington, DC: American Psychological Association Press.

McCabe, A. (1997). Developmental and cross-cultural aspects of children's narration. In M. G. W. Bamberg (Ed.), *Narrative development: Six approaches* (pp. 137–174). Mahwah, NJ: Lawrence Erlbaum.

McCabe, A., & Peterson, A. (1991). *Developing narrative structure.* Hillsdale, NJ: Erlbaum.

Michaels, S. (1991). The dismantling of narrative. In A. McCabe & C. Peterson (Eds.), *Developing narrative structure* (pp. 303–351). Hillsdale, NJ: Erlbaum.

Miller, A. M., & Harwood, R. L. (2002). The cultural organization of parenting: Change and stability of behavior during feeding and social play across the first year of life. *Parenting: Science and Practice, 2*, 241–273.

Miller, J. G. (1994). Cultural psychology: Bridging disciplinary boundaries in understanding the cultural grounding of self. In P. K. Bock (Ed.), *Handbook of psychological anthropology* (pp. 139–170). Westport, CT: Greenwood Press.

Miller, J. G. (1997). Theoretical issues in cultural psychology and social constructionism. In J. W. Berry, Y. Poortinga, & J. Pandey (Eds.), *Handbook of cross-cultural psychology: Vol. 1. Theoretical and methodological perspectives* (2nd ed., pp. 85–128). Boston: Allyn & Bacon.

Miller, P. J. (1982). *Amy, Wendy, and Beth: Learning language in South Baltimore.* Austin, TX: University Press.

Miller, P. J. (1994). Narrative practices: Their role in socialization and self construction. In U. Neisser & R. Fivush (Eds.), *The remembering self: Construction and accuracy in the self-narrative* (pp. 158–179). New York: Cambridge University Press.

Miller, P. J. (1996). Instantiating culture through discourse practices: Some personal reflections on socialization and how to study it. In R. Jessor, A. Colby, & R. Shweder (Eds.), *Ethnography and human development: Context and meaning in social inquiry* (pp. 183–204). Chicago: University of Chicago Press.

Miller, P. J., Cho, G. E., & Bracey, J. (2005). Working-class children's experience through the prism of personal storytelling. *Human Development, 48*, 115–135.

Miller, P. J., Fung, H., & Koven, M. (2007). Narrative reverberations: How participation in narrative practices co-creates persons and cultures. In S. Kitayama & D. Cohen (Eds.), *Handbook of cultural psychology* (pp. 595–614). New York: Guilford Press.

Miller, P. J., Fung, H., & Mintz, J. (1996). Self-construction through narrative practices: A Chinese and American comparison of early socialization. *Ethos, 24*, 1–44.

Miller, P. J., & Goodnow, J. J. (1995). Cultural practices: Toward an integration of culture and development. In J. J. Goodnow, P. J. Miller, & F. Kessel (Eds.), *Cultural practices as contexts for development: New directions for child and adolescent development* (Issue No. 67, pp. 5–16). San Francisco: Jossey-Bass.

Miller, P. J., Hengst, J., Alexander, K. A., & Sperry, L. L. (2000). Narrative genres: Tools for creating alternate realities. In K. Rosengren, C. Johnson, & P. Harris (Eds.), *Imagining the impossible: The development of magical, scientific, and religious thinking in contemporary society*, (pp. 212–246). New York: Cambridge University Press.

Miller, P. J., Hengst, J. A., & Wang, S.-H. (2003). Ethnographic methods: Applications from developmental cultural psychology. In P. M. Camic, J. E. Rhodes, & L. Yardley (Eds.), *Qualitative research in psychology: Expanding perspectives in methodology and design* (pp. 219–242). Washington, DC: American Psychological Association.

Miller, P. J., & Hoogstra, L. (1992). Language as a tool in the socialization and apprehension of cultural meanings. In T. Schwartz, G. M. White, & C. A. Lutz (Eds.), *New directions in psychological anthropology* (pp. 83–101). New York: Cambridge University Press.

Miller, P. J., Hoogstra, L., Mintz, J., Fung, H., & Williams, K. (1993). Troubles in the garden and how they get resolved: A young child's transformation of his favorite story. In C. A. Nelson (Ed.), *Memory and affect in development*. Minnesota symposia on child psychology, Vol. **26**. Hillsdale, NJ: Erlbaum.

Miller, P. J., Koven, M., & Lin, S. (2011). Narrative. In A. Duranti, E. Ochs, & B. B. Schieffelin (Eds.), *Handbook of language socialization* (pp. 190–208). Hoboken, NJ: Wiley-Blackwell Publishers.

Miller, P. J., Mintz, J., Fung, H., Hoogstra, L., & Potts, R. (1992). The narrated self: Young children's construction of self in relation to others in conversational stories of personal experience. *Merrill-Palmer Quarterly, 38*, 45–67.

Miller, P. J., & Moore, B. B. (1989). Narrative conjunctions of caregiver and child: A comparative perspective on socialization through stories. *Ethos, 17*, 43–64.

Miller, P. J., Potts, R., Fung, H., Hoogstra, L., & Mintz, J. (1990). Narrative practices and the social construction of self in childhood. *American Ethnologist, 17*, 97–116.

Miller, P. J., Sandel, T. L., Liang, C.-H., & Fung, H. (2001). Narrating transgressions in Longwood: The discourses, meanings, and paradoxes of an American socializing practice. *Ethos, 29*, 159–186.

Miller, P. J., & Sperry, L. L. (1988). Early talk about the past: The origins of conversational stories of personal experience. *Journal of Child Language, 15*, 293–315.

Miller, P. J., Wang, S.-H., Sandel, T. L., & Cho, G. E. (2002). Self-esteem as folk theory: A comparison of European-American and Taiwanese mothers' beliefs. *Parenting: Science and Practice, 3*, 209–239.

Miller, P. J., Wiley, A. R., Fung, H., & Liang, C.-H. (1997). Personal storytelling as a medium of socialization in Chinese and American families. *Child Development*, **68**, 1557–1568.

Mintz, J. (1999). *The social construction of self-esteem: Narrative discourse practices among parents and preschool children in a middle-class, European-American community.* Unpublished doctoral dissertation, University of Chicago.

Nelson, K. (Ed.) (1989). *Narratives from the crib.* Cambridge: MA: Harvard University Press.

Nelson, K. (1993). Events, narratives, memories: What develops? In C. Nelson (Ed.), *Minnesota symposium on child psychology: Vol. 26. Memory and affect in development* (pp. 1–24). Hillsdale, NJ: Erlbaum.

Nelson, K. (1996). *Language in cognitive development: The emergence of the mediated mind.* New York: Cambridge University Press.

Nelson, K., & Fivush, R. (2004). The Emergence of autobiographical memory: A social cultural developmental theory. *Psychological Review*, **111**, 486–511.

Ochs, E. (1979). Transcription as theory. In E. Ochs & B. B. Schieffelin (Eds.), *Developmental pragmatics* (pp. 43–72). New York: Academic Press.

Ochs, E. (1988). *Culture and language development: Language acquisition and language socialization in a Samoan village.* New York: Cambridge University Press.

Ochs, E. (1990). Indexicality and socialization. In J. W. Stigler, R. A. Shweder, & G. Herdt (Eds.), *Cultural psychology: Essays on comparative human development* (pp. 287–308). Cambridge, MA: Harvard University Press.

Ochs, E. (1991). Linguistic resources for socializing humanity. *Proceedings of the International Symposium on "Rethinking Linguistic Relativity."* Ocho Rios, Jamaica: Wenner-Green Foundation.

Ochs, E. (1999). Socialization. *Journal of Linguistic Anthropology*, **9**, 230–233.

Ochs, E., & Capps, L. (2001). *Living narrative: Creating lives in everyday storytelling.* Cambridge, MA: Harvard University Press.

Ochs, E., & Schieffelin, B. B. (1984). Language acquisition and socialization: Three developmental stories and their implications. In R. A. Shweder & R. A. LeVine (Eds.), *Culture theory: Essays on mind, self and emotion* (pp. 276–320). Cambridge, UK: Cambridge University Press.

Ochs, E., Smith, R., & Taylor, C. E. (1989). Detective stories at dinnertime: Problem-solving through co-narrations. *Cultural Dynamics*, **2**, 238–257.

Ochs, E., & Taylor, C. E. (1992). Family narrative as political activity. *Discourse and Society*, **3**, 301–340.

Ochs, E., & Taylor, C. E. (1995). The "father knows best" dynamic in dinnertime conversation. In K. Hall & M. Bueholtz (Eds.), *Gender articulated* (pp. 97–120). New York: Routledge.

Ortner, S. B. (1984). Theory of anthropology since the sixties. *Comparative Studies in Society and History*, **126**, 126–66.

Peterson, C. (2004). Mothers, fathers, and gender: Parental narratives about children. *Narrative Inquiry*, **14**, 323–346.

Pike, K. L. (1967). *Language in relation to a unified theory of the structure of human behavior.* The Hague, The Netherlands: Mouton.

Pratt, M. W., & Fiese, B. H. (Eds.). (2004). *Family stories and the life course: Across time and generations.* Mahwah, NJ: Erlbaum.

Qiao, Q., & Ma, T. Y. (1973). *President Chiang Kai-Shek and the renaissance of Chinese culture.* Taipei, Taiwan: Wuchow Publishing Co. [in Chinese]

Quas, J., & Fivush, R. (Eds.). (2009). *Emotion in memory and development: Biological, cognitive, and social considerations.* New York: Oxford University Press.

Quinn, N. (Ed.). (2005a). *Finding culture in talk: A collection of methods.* New York: Palgrave Macmillan.

Quinn, N. (2005b). Universals of child rearing. *Anthropological Theory,* **5**(4), 477–516.

Rogoff, B. (1990). *Apprenticeship in thinking: Cognitive development in social context.* New York: Oxford University Press.

Rogoff, B. (2003). *The cultural nature of human development.* New York: Oxford University Press.

Rogoff, B., Mistry, J., Göncü, A., Mosier, C., Chavajay, P., & Heath, S. B. (1993). Guided participation in cultural activity by toddlers and caregivers. *Monographs of the Society for Research in Child Development,* **58**(8, Serial No. 236). Malden, MA: Wiley-Blackwell Publishers.

Rogoff, B., Moore, L., Najafi, B., Dexter, A., Correa-Chavez, M., & Solis, J. (2007). Children's development of cultural repertoires through participation in everyday routines and practices. In J. E. Grusec & P. D. Hastings (Eds.), *Handbook of socialization: Theory and research* (pp. 490–515). New York: Guilford Press.

Rogoff, B., Paradise, R., Arauz, R. M., Correa-Chavez, M., & Angelillo, C. (2003). Firsthand learning through intent participation. *Annual Review Psychology,* **54**, 175–203.

Sandel, T. L. (2003). Linguistic capital in Taiwan: The KMT's Mandarin language policy and its perceived impact on language practices of bilingual Mandarin and Tai-gi speakers. *Language in Society,* **32**, 523–551.

Savani, K., Markus, H. R., & Conner, A. L. (2008). Let your preference be your guide? Preferences and choices are more tightly linked for North Americans than for Indians. *Journal of Personality and Social Psychology,* **95**, 861–876.

Schieffelin, B. B. (1990). *The give and take of everyday life: Language socialization of Kaluli children.* New York: Cambridge University Press.

Schieffelin, B. B., & Ochs, E. (1986). *Language socialization across cultures.* New York: Cambridge University Press.

Scollon, R., & Scollon, S. B. K. (1981). *Narrative, literacy, and face in interethnic communication.* Norwood, NJ: Ablex Publishing Corporation.

Shweder, R. A. (1991). *Thinking through culture: Expeditions in cultural psychology.* Cambridge, MA: Harvard University Press.

Shweder, R. A., Bidell, T., Dailey, A., Dixon, S., Miller, P. J., & Modell, J. (Eds.). (2009). *The child: An encyclopedic companion.* Chicago: University of Chicago Press.

Shweder, R. A., Goodnow, J. J., Hatano, G., LeVine, R. A., Markus, H., & Miller, P. J. (2006). The cultural psychology of development: One mind, many mentalities. In W. Damon (Series Ed.) & R. M. Lerner (Vol. Ed.), *Handbook of child psychology: Vol. 1. Theoretical models of human development* (6th ed., pp. 716–792). New York: Wiley.

Shweder, R. A., & Much, N. C. (1987). Determinations of meaning: Discourse and moral socialization. In W. M. Kurtines & J. L. Gewirtz (Eds.), *Moral development through social interaction* (pp. 197–244). New York: John Wiley & Sons.

Silverstein, M. (1976/1995). Shifters, linguistic categories, and cultural description. In B. Blount (Ed.), *Language, culture, and society: A book of readings* (pp. 187–221). Prospect Heights, IL: Waveland Press.

Silverstein, M. (1981). The limits of awareness. Working papers in sociolinguistics 84. Austin, TX: Southwest Educational Development Laboratory.

Simon, D. F., & Kau, M. Y. M. (1992). *Taiwan: Beyond the economic miracle.* Armonk, NY: M. E. Sharpe.

Sperry, L. L., & Sperry, D. E. (1996). Early development of narrative skills. *Cognitive Development,* **11**, 443–465.

Sperry, L. L., & Sperry, D. E. (2000). Verbal and nonverbal contributions to early representation: Evidence from African–American toddlers. In N. Budwig, I. C. Uzgiris, & J.

V. Wertsch (Eds.), *Communication: An arena of development* (pp. 143–165). Norwood, NJ: Ablex.

Stevenson, H. W., Lee, S. Y., Chen, C., Stigler, J. W., Hsu, C. C., & Kitamura, S. (1990). Contexts of achievement: A study of American, Chinese, and Japanese children. *Monographs of the Society for Research in Child Development*, **55**(1–2, Serial No. 221, pp. 1–119).

Stevenson, H. W., & Stigler, J. W. (1992). *The learning gap: Why our schools are failing and what we can learn from Japanese and Chinese education*. New York: Summit Books.

Su, Y. C. (2006). Political ideology and Taiwan school curricula. *Asia Pacific Education Review*, **7**, 41–50.

Tamis-LeMonda, C. S., Wang, S., Koutsouvanou, E., & Albright, M. (2002). Childrearing values in Greece, Taiwan, and the United States. *Parenting: Science and Practice*, **2**, 185–208.

Taylor, C. (1989). *Sources of the self: The making of the modern identity*. Cambridge, MA: Harvard University Press.

Taylor, C. E. (1995). "You think it was a fight?": Co-constructing (the struggle for) meaning, face, and family in everyday narrative activity. *Research on Language and Social Interaction*, **28**(3), 283–317.

Thorne, B. (1993). *Gender play: Girls and boys in school*. New Brunswck, NJ: Rutgers University Press.

Tobin, J. (1995). The irony of self-expression. *American Journal of Education*, **103**, 233–258.

Van Deusen-Phillips, S. B., Goldin-Meadow, S., & Miller, P. J. (2001). Enacting stories, seeing worlds: Similarities and differences in the cross-cultural narrative development of linguistically isolated deaf children. *Human Development*, **44**, 311–336.

Vygotsky, L. S. (1934/1978). In M. Cole, V. John-Steiner, S. Scribner, & E. Souberman (Eds.), *Mind in society: The development of higher psychological processes*. Cambridge, MA: Harvard University Press.

Wachman, A. M. (1994). Competing identities in Taiwan. In M. A. Rubinstein (Ed.), *The other Taiwan: 1945 to present* (pp. 18–80). New York: M. E. Sharpe.

Wang, Q., & Leichtman, M. D. (2000). Same beginnings, different stories: A comparison of American and Chinese children's narratives. *Child Development*, **71**, 1329–1346.

Wang, Q., Leichtman, M. D., & Davies, K. I. (2000). Sharing memories and telling stories: American and Chinese mothers and their 3-year-olds. *Memory*, **8**, 159–178.

Wang, X-L., Bernas, R., & Eberhard, P. (2008). Responding to children's everyday transgressions in Chinese working-class families. *Journal of Moral Education*, **37**, 55–79.

Wang, Y. Z., Wiley, A. R., & Zhou, X. (2007). The effect of different cultural lenses on reliability and validity in observational data: The example of Chinese immigrant parent–toddler dinner interactions. *Social Development*, **16**, 777–799.

Watson-Gegeo, K. A., & Gegeo D. W. (1990). Shaping the mind and straightening out conflicts: The discourse of Kwara'ae family counseling. In K. A. Watson-Gegeo & G. M. White (Eds.), *Disentangling: Conflict discourse in Pacific societies* (pp. 161–213). Stanford, CA: Stanford University Press.

Watson-Gegeo, K. A., & Gegeo, D. W. (1999). Remodeling culture in Kwara'ae: The role of discourse in children's cognitive development. *Discourse Studies*, **1**, 227–245.

Weisner, T. S. (1996). Why ethnography should be the most important method in the study of human development. In R. Jessor, A. Colby, & R. Shweder (Eds.), *Ethnography and human development: Context and meaning in social inquiry* (pp. 305–324). Chicago: University of Chicago Press.

Weisner, T. S. (2002). Ecocultural pathways, family values, and parenting. *Parenting: Science and Practice*, **2**, 325–334.

Weisner, T. S. (Ed.). (2005). *Discovering successful pathways in children's development: Mixed methods in the study of childhood and family life.* Chicago: University of Chicago Press.

Wertsch, J. V. (1985). *Vygotsky and the social formation of mind.* Cambridge, MA: Harvard University Press.

Wertsch, J. V. (1991). *Voices of the mind: A sociocultural approach to mediated action.* Cambridge, MA: Harvard University Press.

Wiley, A. R., Rose, A. J., Burger, L. K., & Miller, P. J. (1998). The construction of autonomy through narrative practices: A comparative study of working-class and middle-class families. *Child Development, 69,* 833–847.

Wolcott, H. F. (1995). *The art of fieldwork.* Walnut Creek, CA: AltaMira Press.

Wolf, M. (1992). *A thrice told tale: Feminism, postmodernism, and ethnographic responsibility.* Stanford, CA: Stanford University Press.

Wu, D. Y. H. (1981). Child abuse in Taiwan. In J. E. Korbin (Ed.), *Child abuse and neglect: Cross-cultural perspectives* (pp. 139–165). Berkeley: University of California Press.

Wu, D. Y. H. (1996). Chinese childhood socialization. In M. H. Bond (Ed.), *The handbook of Chinese psychology* (pp. 143–154). Hong Kong: Oxford University Press.

Yum, J. O. (1991). The impact of Confucianism on interpersonal relationships and communication patterns in East Asia. In L. A. Samovar & R. E. Porter (Eds.), *Intercultural communication: A reader* (pp. 66–78). Belmont, CA: Wadsworth.

ACKNOWLEDGMENTS

Peggy Miller acknowledges with gratitude The Spencer Foundation, which provided support for the fieldwork, data collection, and initial analyses for this project and the Chiang Ching-Kuo Foundation, which provided support for analyses of the longitudinal data. Heidi Fung wishes to thank the National Science Council and Academia Sinica for the research grants and awards provided by them in the past years. We are grateful to the anonymous reviewers for their cogent suggestions for improving the manuscript. We thank Judith Mintz for her ethnographic work in Longwood. We are grateful to the undergraduate students from the Departments of Communication and Psychology at the University of Illinois who helped to transcribe and analyze the data; this work would not have come to fruition without their contribution. We thank Megan Olivarez for her expert assistance in the preparation of the manuscript. Most of all, we thank the Taipei and Longwood families for welcoming us into their homes and participating in a demanding study.

CONTRIBUTORS

Peggy J. Miller is Professor of Communication and Professor of Psychology at the University of Illinois at Urbana-Champaign. She has published extensively on socialization through everyday talk in diverse communities, with a focus on cultural and social class comparisons. Her research is interdisciplinary, drawing upon developmental psychology, cultural psychology, communication studies, and anthropology. In 2006–2007, she was a Fellow at the Radcliffe Institute for Advanced Study, Harvard University. She is the author of *Amy, Wendy, and Beth: Learning Language in South Baltimore*, a co-author of *"Raise up a Child": Human Development in an African-American Family* and a co-editor of *The Child: An Encyclopedic Companion*. She is currently studying self-esteem as a cultural ideal and childrearing goal that circulates widely in contemporary American society.

Heidi Fung is a Research Fellow at the Institute of Ethnology, Academia Sinica, Taipei, Taiwan. She received her doctoral training in the Committee on Human Development at the University of Chicago. She was a visiting scholar at the Yenching Institute and the Graduate School of Education at Harvard University in 2000–2001. She has long been interested in how to situate human development in socio-cultural contexts. Her research involves the socialization of emotion, daily disciplinary and moral training practices, and childrearing beliefs across cultures. Recently, she conducted fieldwork in Taiwan and Vietnam to explore how socialization and family ties are practiced across borders and across generations by Vietnamese marriage migrants in Taiwan.

Shumin Lin is a Postdoctoral Fellow in the Department of Anthropology at the University of South Florida. She received her Ph.D. in 2009 from the Department of Educational Psychology at the University of Illinois at Urbana-Champaign. Her dissertation was entitled *Education at Last! Taiwanese Grandmothers "Go to School."* She is committed to understanding the role language plays in the processes of socialization across the lifespan and in the construction of social inequality. She approaches these problems from an interdisciplinary standpoint, drawing upon linguistic anthropology, cultural

127

psychology, sociolinguistics, and communication. Her main research program examines elderly minority speakers' experiences of linguistic marginalization through their participation in contemporary communicative milieus in media consumption, senior adult education, and intergenerational communication.

Eva Chian-Hui Chen is Assistant Professor in the Department of Psychology at the Benedictine College in Kansas. She received her Ph.D. in developmental psychology in 2011 from the University of Illinois at Urbana-Champaign. Prior to embarking on her graduate study in the United States, she worked as a research assistant to Dr. Fung at the Institute of Ethnology, Academia Sinica, Taipei, Taiwan. Her research focuses on children's socialization and women's lives in the context of transnational marriage families. Her dissertation was entitled *Taiwanese-Vietnamese Transnational Marriage Families in Taiwan: Perspectives from Vietnamese Immigrant Mothers and Taiwanese Teachers.*

Benjamin R. Boldt earned his B.S. degree from the University of Illinois at Urbana-Champaign with a double major in Psychology and Molecular and Cellular Biology. Graduating with high honors, he was also the recipient of the 2007 Outstanding Undergraduate Award for research excellence in developmental psychology.

STATEMENT OF EDITORIAL POLICY

The SRCD *Monographs* series aims to publish major reports of developmental research that generates authoritative new findings and that foster a fresh perspective and/or integration of data/research on conceptually significant issues. Submissions may consist of individually or group-authored reports of findings from some single large-scale investigation or from a series of experiments centering on a particular question. Multiauthored sets of independent studies concerning the same underlying question also may be appropriate. A critical requirement in such instances is that the individual authors address common issues and that the contribution arising from the set as a whole be unique, substantial, and well integrated. Manuscripts reporting interdisciplinary or multidisciplinary research on significant developmental questions and those including evidence from diverse cultural, racial, and ethnic groups are of particular interest. Also of special interest are manuscripts that bridge basic and applied developmental science, and that reflect the international perspective of the Society. Because the aim of the *Monographs* series is to enhance cross-fertilization among disciplines or subfields as well as advance knowledge on specialized topics, the links between the specific issues under study and larger questions relating to developmental processes should emerge clearly and be apparent for both general readers and specialists on the topic. In short, irrespective of how it may be framed, work that contributes significant data and/or extends a developmental perspective will be considered.

Potential authors who may be unsure whether the manuscript they are planning would make an appropriate submission to the SRCD *Monographs* are invited to draft an outline or prospectus of what they propose and send it to the incoming editor for review and comment.

Potential authors are not required to be members of the Society for Research in Child Development nor affiliated with the academic discipline of psychology to submit a manuscript for consideration by the *Monographs*. The significance of the work in extending developmental theory and in contributing new empirical information is the crucial consideration.

Submissions should contain a minimum of 80 manuscript pages (including tables and references). The upper boundary of 150–175 pages is more flexible, but authors should try to keep within this limit. If color artwork is submitted, and the authors believe color art is necessary to the presentation of their work, the submissions letter should indicate that one or more authors or their institutions are prepared to pay the substantial costs associated with color art reproduction. Please submit manuscripts electronically to the SRCD Monographs Online Submissions and Review Site (Scholar One) at http://mc.manuscriptcentral.com/mono. Please contact the Monographs office with any questions at monographs@srcd.org.

The corresponding author for any manuscript must, in the submission letter, warrant that all coauthors are in agreement with the content of the manuscript. The corresponding author also is responsible for informing all coauthors, in a timely manner, of manuscript submission, editorial decisions, reviews received, and any revisions recommended. Before publication, the corresponding author must warrant in the submissions letter that the study has been conducted according to the ethical guidelines of the Society for Research in Child Development.

A more detailed description of all editorial policies, evaluation processes, and format requirements, is given in the "Guidelines for the Preparation of Publication Submissions," which can be found at the SRCD website by clicking on *Monographs*, or by contacting the editor.

Monographs Editorial Office
e-mail: monographs@srcd.org

Incoming Editor, Patricia J. Bauer
Department of Psychology, Emory University
36 Eagle Row
Atlanta, GA 30322
e-mail: pjbauer@emory.edu

Note to NIH Grantees

Pursuant to NIH mandate, Society through Wiley-Blackwell will post the accepted version of Contributions authored by NIH grantholders to PubMed Central upon acceptance. This accepted version will be made publicly available 12 months after publication. For further information, see http://www.wiley.com/go/nihmandate.

narratives
    early socialization and, 1–2, 5–6, 11, 106–107
    genres of, 1–2
    as medium of socialization (tool of socialization), 1–2, 5, 105, 108, 110
    of personal experience (*See* personal storytelling)
narrative practices, 1–2, 4–6, 10, 12–13, 24, 53, 57, 59, 90–91, 104–105, 107, 109–110, 113
    navigation of stories, children's, 77–104
    at age 2^1/$_2$-baseline
        Longwood children, 91–93
        Taipei children, 78–81
    at age 3
        Longwood children, 93–95
        Taipei children, 81–84
    at age 3^1/$_2$
        Longwood children, 95–97
        Taipei children, 84–86
    at age 4
        Longwood children, 97–102
        Taipei children, 86–91
    differences in, 103–104
    similarities of, 102–103
new topic, as story ending, 35

observing
    cultural variation in, 13
    within home, methods for, 19–20
    as learning mode, 112
occasioning transgressions
    coding of, 33–34
    opportunity education and, 8, 55,110
    as prompt for narrating past transgressions, 33–34, 49
    rates/frequency of, 36t, 38
opportunity education, 8, 55, 110
outliers, 49

pacifier habit, transgression story of,49–51
parents. *See also* childrearing; Longwood families; Taipei families; fathers; mothers)
participant recruitment, for study, 19
participant roles
    of children, 12–13, 59–76
        age-related patterns in, 61, 62t
        bystanders (*See* bystander role)
        changes over time in children's active participation, 63–66, 67t, 68–71, 71t

CURRENT